new thai cuisine

new thai cuisine

nathan hyam

Whitecap Books

Edited by Elaine Jones
Proofread by Elizabeth McLean
Photographs by Greg Athans
Food styling by Nathan Fong
Food styling assistance by Antoinette Posehn
Cover design by Maxine Lea
Interior design and illustrations by Warren Clark

Printed and bound in Canada

National Library of Canada Cataloguing in Publication Data

Hyam, Nathan, 1951–
    New Thai cuisine

Includes index.
ISBN 1-55285-185-0

    1. Cookery, Thai. I. Title.
TX724.5.T5H92 2001   641.59593   C2001-910382-4

The publisher acknowledges the support of the Canada Council for the
Arts and the Cultural Services Branch of the Government of British
Columbia for our publishing program. We acknowledge the financial
support of the Government of Canada through the Book Publishing
Industry Development Program for our publishing activities.

Contents

Acknowledgments x

Introduction 1

Curry Pastes, Sauces and Broths 7

Red Curry Paste 8
Green Curry Paste 9
Panaeng Curry Paste 10
Massaman Curry Paste 11
Roasted Chili Paste 12
Creamy Peanut Sauce 13
  Pineapple Peanut Sauce 14
  Thai Hoisin Peanut Sauce 15
  Tamarind Peanut Sauce 16
  Sweet Hot Tamarind Sauce 16
  Coconut Ginger Sauce 17
  Honey Lime Sauce 17
  Yellow Curry Sauce 18
  Nam Pla Prig 18
  Dipping Sauce for Dumplings 19
  Apricot Ginger Dipping Sauce 20
  Green Peppercorn Dip 20
  Quick Sweet and Sour Chili Sauce 21
  Sweet Chili Sauce 22
  Ginger Cream Sauce 23
  Smoked Oyster Coconut Sauce 24
  Thai Chicken Stock 25
  Lemon Grass Broth 26

Appetizers 27

Minced Chicken and Water Chestnut Dumplings 28
Khanom Krok Coconut Dumplings 29
Duck and Mushroom Potstickers with Apricot Ginger Dipping Sauce 30
Spinach and Mushroom Potstickers 31
Sweet Corn Patties 32
Fish and Vegetable Patties 33
Yam and Sesame Patties 34
Spicy Street Satay 35
Pork Satay 36
Coconut Marinated Chicken Satay 37
Spinach and Peanut Dip 38
Thai Spring Rolls 39
Barbecued Duck and Mushroom Fresh Spring Rolls 40
Northern Thai Whiskey-Marinated Chicken Wings 41
Chicken Wings in Lemon Grass Red Wine Sauce 42
Herbed and Sweetened Prawns 43
Lettuce Wraps 44
Leaf-wrapped Rice Noodles with Savories 45
Sanit's Sweet Chili Dip for Green Mango 46

Soups 47

Thai Roasted Vegetable and Chicken Soup 48
Thai Shrimp and Jasmine Rice Soup 49
Chicken and Coconut Milk Soup 50
Tom Yam Prawn Soup 51
Tom Yam Chicken Soup 52
Coriander Broth with Prawn and Pork Dumplings 53
Herbed Prawn and Vegetable Soup 54
Salmon, Tamarind and Ginger Soup 55
Vegetarian Tom Yam Soup 56
Country-Style Hot and Sour Soup 57

Salads 59

Chicken, Prawn and Fruit Salad 60
Chopped Chicken Salad 61
Southern Thai Bean Thread Noodle and Chicken Salad 62
Northern Thai Shrimp Salad 63
Lemon Grass Beef Salad 64
Green Bean Salad with Coconut Milk Dressing 65
Som Tam Green Papaya Salad 66
Peanut Sesame Noodle Salad 67
Keow's Roasted Eggplant Salad 68
Cucumber Chili Salad 69

Fish and Seafood 71

Salmon in Rice Paper Wraps with Coconut Ginger Sauce 72
Salmon Baked in Banana Leaves 73
Roasted Rock Fish with Coconut and Mango 74
Monkfish in Green Coconut Curry Sauce 75
Grilled Pomfret with Tamarind Chili Sauce 76
Grilled Squid with Tamarind Chili Sauce 77
Baa Wan's Squid Stir-fry 78
Red Snapper and Prawns in Lemon Grass Coconut Curry Sauce 79
Chili Garlic Prawns with Asparagus 80
Tiger Prawns with Thai Herb Pesto Sauce 81
Prawns with Ginger Cream Sauce 82
Phuket Prawns 83
Lemon Grass Curried Mussels 84
Seared Scallops and Basil Mango Sauce 85
Whiskey and Coconut Marinated Seared Scallops 86
Steamed Seafood Custard 87

Poultry 89

Lime and Honey Roasted Duck 90
Pineapple Chicken and Cashews in Banana Leaves 91
Massaman Chicken Curry 92
Lime and Tamarind Chicken 93

Poultry (Cont.)

Chicken and Red Peppers in Red Coconut Curry Sauce 94
Rama Spinach Chicken Curry 95
Roasted Chili Paste Chicken and Peanuts in Banana Leaves 96
Spicy Mint Chicken 97
Northern-Style Marinated Chicken with Sweet Tomato Chutney 98
Spicy Chicken, Basil and Pepper Stir-fry 99
Thai Whiskey Peppercorn Marinated Chicken 100
Spicy Cilantro Roast Chicken with Honey Lime Sauce 101
Coconut Lemon Grass Baked Chicken 102
Herb Glazed Chicken 103
Chicken and Mushrooms in Green Coconut Curry 104
Coconut Curry Chicken with Ginger and Eggplant 105
Peanut Sesame Orange Chicken 106

Vegetables 107

Vegetables in Lemon Grass Broth 108
Mushroom Satay 109
Rachini's Mushroom Stir-fry 110
Eggplant Stuffed with Coconut and Cilantro 111
Eggplant and Potato in Green Coconut Curry Sauce 112
Stir-fried Spinach with Salted Soybeans 113
Curried Spinach with Tofu and Cashews 114
Chili Garlic Beans with Cashews 115
Coconut-Lime Green Beans and Bamboo Shoots 116
Stir-fried Red Curry Mango Vegetables 117
Curried Vegetables in Banana Leaves 118
Bean Sprout and Scallion Stir-fry 119
Thai Basil and Sweet Corn 120

Rice and Noodles 121

Jasmine Rice 122
Thai Black or Red Rice 122
Ginger-Infused Toasted Coconut Jasmine Rice 123
Lemon Grass Risotto 124

Pineapple Fried Rice 125
Chicken and Cashew Fried Rice 126
Tiger Prawn and Basil Fried Rice 127
Ginger and Mushroom Baked Coconut Rice 128
Egg Noodles with Thai Herb Pesto 129
Chiang Mai Noodles 130
Shiitake Mushroom Rice Noodle Stir-fry 131
Bangkok Coconut Rice Noodles 132
Drunkard's Noodles 133
Bangkok Street Vendor Rice Noodle Stir-fry 134
Dried Shrimp (or Chicken) Paad Thai 135
Tiger Prawn Paad Thai 136
Chicken and Snow Peas with Curry Cream Pasta 137

Desserts 139

Mango Lime Sauce 140
Banana Whiskey Cream Sauce 140
Banana Lime Sauté 141
Sticky Rice and Mango 142
Sticky Rice and Banana Grilled in Banana Leaves 143
Tropical Trifle 144
Coconut Cream Pudding 145
Gingered Black Rice Pudding 146
Banana Coconut Candy 147
Banana Ginger Squares 148
Coconut Ginger Chocolate Brownies 149
Banana Mango Cake 150
Chocolate Banana Coconut Cake 151
Mango Cream Tarts 152

Glossary of Thai Ingredients 153

Mail Order Sources for Thai Ingredients 158

Index 159

About the Author 166

Acknowledgments

I would like to express my appreciation to the many Thai cooks who generously shared the love of their culture and food with me. They were all excited about my interest in Thai cooking and showed me the vast spectrum of their cuisine with enthusiasm and laughter. These memories inspire me.

I want to thank my Fraser Valley friends for turning cooking and eating into a joyous occasion and my friend Sean for convincing me that exploring the planet can be more fulfilling than job seniority.

I also want my wife, Faye, to know I am grateful for her unending support and encouragement, and the patience she showed while waiting in numerous restaurant dining rooms throughout Southeast Asia while I communed with the chefs.

Introduction

How does a chef born in New York City come to be known as the Thai guy? It happened about 10 years ago after a grueling 2 years starting the Picasso café restaurant training program in Vancouver, British Columbia, for youth "at risk." My wife and I were both ready for a sabbatical.

We pictured returning to Portugal and Spain for a few months and poking around in the small fishing villages, reliving fond memories, or maybe visiting the blue lagoons of the Yucatan. We could stay in a palapa hut by the Caribbean and practice cooking chicken in banana leaves while sipping the local Leon Negra dark beer.

We were trying to figure out where we could stay the longest before finances would force our return when our friends Bob and Joanne said, "Why not go somewhere you've never been?" They had been staying in Southeast Asia every winter for years and told stories of hotel rooms for 5 dollars and great meals for 75 cents, miles of empty white sand beaches and warm tropical waters. It sounded too good to be true, but they gave us their journal to read, an account of their last trip to Thailand, Malaysia and Indonesia.

That journal changed our lives. It was a fascinating, hilarious peek at the mysterious Orient and after reading about their saga, we booked two seats to Bangkok and were off on our own adventure.

A decade later, after many Thai cooking courses, mentoring by Thai chefs and more travels in Asia, I am still passionate about Thai cuisine and feel the constant tug of the "kingdom of smiles" pulling me back.

A Little History

Thai cookery is a cuisine that has developed a rich complexity over many centuries. Thailand is unique in Southeast Asia in that it is free of a colonial past, so the influences on the cuisine occurred naturally, slowly and by choice. The Thai people are always open to new culinary ideas and have adapted ingredients and techniques from other cultures and made them an integral part of their daily lives. The cuisine has been affected by neighbors in Vietnam, Malaysia and Indonesia, but the three countries that have had the most profound effect are China, India and Portugal.

The influence from China can be seen in the use of the wok, stir-fry tools and ingredients such as soy sauce, oyster sauce, tofu, sesame oil and noodles. Thai cooks found new ways to use these products, and although all Thai noodle dishes are credited as originating in China, the flavors in a dish like Paad Thai are something you will not find in any other cuisine.

The threads leading back to India are evident in Thai curries. Curry powder is not a spice but a blend of up to 25 different dried spices. When Thais saw how Indian traders who landed on the coasts prepared their curries, the cooks of the day took that idea and created new dishes. They used the dried spices, but they added fresh local ingredients, like lemon grass, shallots, garlic, galanga and chilies. Instead of the yogurt common in Indian curries, they used coconut milk to mellow the spices. A new Thai tradition was born.

Many people are surprised to hear that Portugal had a role to play in developing the

1

flavors of Thai cuisine. Chilies are a common ingredient in Thai food, but chilies did not grow in Asia before the 1500s, when the Portuguese, after discovering chilies in Africa, spread their use throughout the Asian world. The Thai people had always had a spicy food tradition, but before sailors from Portugal arrived, they used black, white and green peppercorns to spice up their dishes. Another significant contribution from the Portuguese was the use of sugar and eggs for desserts. This can be seen in a dessert like the traditional coconut custard, which is based on the Portuguese Pudim Flan (crème caramel).

Global traditions continue to influence Thai cuisine. Many Thai chefs have had successful restaurants in the West and have returned to Thailand with an understanding of Western techniques and ingredients. This has resulted in a fusion of culinary styles sometimes referred to as modern Thai cuisine. Many of the dishes throughout the book fall into this category.

No book about Thai food could overlook the street vendors. Every city in Thailand has numerous street vendors—Bangkok alone is said to have about 25,000. When a person migrates from the countryside to a large urban area they often sell food specialties from their village to support themselves. Patronizing the street vendors is an excellent way to get an overview of Thai regional cuisines. Many residents of large cities in Thailand never cook at home because the street food is inexpensive and high quality. The vendors usually stay in the same location and people in the neighborhood become part of the family. This creates a village atmosphere in the heart of a bustling city. Many of the recipes in this book are versions of street food.

The Philosophy of Thai Cuisine

Thai cuisine is an art form, rather than a rigid set of rules. To succeed requires some understanding of the basic techniques and practice. The goal is not to take a scientific approach to measurements, but to allow room for personal creativity in the cooking process.

I have heard Thai chefs say that cooking is similar to meditation. You need calm and focus to create a perfect meal. So relax and smile while you are in the kitchen.

The word most often used in Thailand to describe the flavors in a traditional meal is harmony. Herbs, spices, roots and aromatic leaves are carefully blended to enhance the natural flavors and textures of the main ingredients.

Variety, texture and color are important aspects of any Thai meal. Many texture and flavor contrasts, such as soft and crunchy, and sweet, sour, bitter, salty and spicy (hot), are typically included as elements in a meal.

Armed with this philosophical approach, the next step is choosing and using a recipe. Remember that a recipe is a basic guideline; to get the most out of it, consider it merely a jumping-off point. The most important piece of equipment in your kitchen is your tasting spoon. Always taste your food as it cooks so you can decide how to adjust the flavors.

Pick any traditional Thai dish and you will find hundreds of versions of it in different homes and restaurants throughout the country. This was one of the most fascinating discoveries I made as I traveled the countryside, wheedling my way into people's kitchens. Most cooks were eager to show me their own version of a dish, always followed by a description of how an aunt makes it up north or how mom makes it in the home village. I never tasted the same red coconut curry in any two different homes. Thai people see this personal interpretation and diversity as a positive thing. The basic premise is that it's the ingredients and technique that make a Thai dish authentic, not a particular recipe.

With this thought in mind, I suggest you follow the measurements exactly the first time you make these recipes. When the dish is finished, analyze the flavors. Was it too hot? Did it have enough garlic for your taste? The next few times you make the recipe continue to taste critically and make flavor adjustments. Eventually you will reach the balance that is perfect for you. When this has happened, you will have your own authentic recipe.

Taste is very subjective. No one else can decide what tastes good to you, so be bold, experiment and give yourself permission to enjoy your time in the kitchen. You will learn what you don't like from making mistakes, but more often than not you will learn what works for you. Some of the greatest recipes came about because a cook tried something that was not in the rulebook. If you are willing to have fun and experiment, your creative potential will be limitless.

The Thai Meal

Food in Thailand, as it is in France, is not just for nourishment. Most Thais think of food as a subject of incredible interest and endless discussion. It is art, history and a reason to enjoy the company of friends.

Lunch in Thailand is often a simple affair—fried rice or noodles. The evening meal, however, can be an elaborate production.

Everyone at the table is served rice—the foundation of every meal. The rest of the dishes are served, all at the same time, on platters. Each person takes a little food from each dish and places it on their plate.

Thai people use only a tablespoon and a fork at the table. The spoon is what people use to eat with and the fork is used to push food onto the spoon. Knives are considered inappropriate at the table. This stems from ancient times when knives were carried as weapons. It would be impolite to use a weapon to eat with, so, as in Chinese cuisine, food is prepared in bite-size pieces. If something needs to be cut smaller at the table, the side of the spoon is used. Thai people only use chopsticks to eat noodles.

When planning a menu, the two underlying principles are using a variety of textures and using the full spectrum of flavors: sweet, salty, bitter, spicy (hot) and sour. A typical meal would include a clear soup, a curry, a deep-fried or stir-fried dish and a spicy salad.

Following are several suggestions for menus. These are combinations that I have used, but there are many more possibilities. There is only one rule for combining dishes in a meal that makes sense: if it tastes good to you, it is the right combination.

— 1 —

Tom Yam Prawn Soup (p. 51)
Spinach and Peanut Dip with
Sliced Vegetables (p. 38)
Grilled Squid with Tamarind Chili Sauce (p. 77)
Chicken and Red Peppers in
Red Coconut Curry Sauce (p. 94)
Ginger and Mushroom Baked Coconut Rice (p. 128)
Thai Stir-fried Vegetables (p. 117 or 119)
Fresh tropical fruit

— 2 —

Som Tam Green Papaya Salad (p. 66)
Coriander Broth with Prawn and
Pork Dumplings (p. 53)
Red Snapper and Prawns in
Lemon Grass Coconut Curry Sauce (p. 79)
Thai Whiskey Peppercorn Marinated Chicken with
Sweet Chili Sauce (p. 100)
Jasmine Rice (p. 122)
Banana Lime Sauté (p. 141)

— 3 —

Coconut Marinated Chicken Satay (p. 37)
with Creamy Peanut Sauce (p. 13)
Sweet Corn Patties with Sweet Chili Sauce (p. 32)
Monkfish in Green Coconut Curry Sauce (p. 75)
Stir-fried Spinach with Salted Soybeans (p. 113)
Jasmine Rice (p. 122)
Banana Ginger Squares (p. 148)

— 4 —

Pork Satay (p. 36)
with Pineapple Peanut Sauce (p. 14)
Vegetarian Tom Yam Soup (p. 56)
Whiskey and Coconut Marinated
Seared Scallops (p. 86)
Lime and Honey Roasted Duck (p. 90)
Lemon Grass Risotto (p. 124)
Coconut-Lime Green Beans
and Bamboo Shoots (p. 116)
Mango Cream Tarts (p. 152)

— 5 —

Lemon Grass Beef Salad (p. 64)
Salmon, Tamarind and Ginger Soup (p. 55)
Coconut Curry Chicken
with Ginger and Eggplant (p. 105)
Vegetables in Lemon Grass Broth (p. 108)
Ginger-Infused Toasted Coconut
Jasmine Rice (p. 123)
Banana Coconut Candy (p. 147)

— 6 —

Lettuce Wraps (p. 44)
Pork Satay (p. 36)
Chili Garlic Prawns with Asparagus (p.80)
Massaman Chicken Curry (p. 92)
Bean Sprout and Scallion Stir-fry (p. 119)
Pineapple Fried Rice (p. 125)
Chocolate Banana Coconut Cake (p. 151)

Some Practical Tips

Basic Stir-fry Techniques

The flavor, texture and color of many Thai dishes depend on quick cooking at *very* high heat. This seals in the juices, flavors and nutritional value of all the ingredients. Most dishes can be made in a skillet or a saucepan, but the shape of a wok makes it the best choice for stir-fry. Its curved sides produce graduated temperature zones that allow you to cook many different ingredients without having to remove them from the wok. Food that is cooked is pushed up the sloped sides of the wok to keep warm, allowing room to stir-fry other ingredients on the bottom cooking surface.

When purchasing a wok, it is important to consider the metal it is made from. Carbon steel or cast-iron woks are ideal because they conduct heat evenly. If seasoned properly and dried after washing they will last for years. Stainless steel is a very poor heat conductor and these woks will have hot and cold spots that cause food to stick and burn. Non-stick coated woks are inappropriate for stir-frying because non-stick cookware is designed for low heat cooking; if used at the high temperatures required for stir-frying the coating will peel off.

Following are some tips for successful stir-frying.

- Have everything ready before you start cooking.
- Slice all the ingredients into similar shapes and sizes to ensure that everything cooks at the same rate. Group items with similar cooking times together. For instance, place carrots and cilantro in two separate groups.
- Use an oil with a high smoking point. The smoke point of an oil refers to the temperature at which it will start to break down and fill your kitchen with smoke. Peanut and canola oil have high smoke points and are ideal for stir-frying, while olive oil and butter will not work at the necessary temperatures.
- Preheat the wok on high heat for about a minute. Add the oil and let it heat for 15 seconds before adding the onion, garlic and ginger to flavor the oil. Cook for about 1 minute and remove from the oil if required in the recipe.
- Stir-fry the meat first, just until the color changes, then remove it from the wok. Cook the vegetables next, starting with the firmer ones and progressing to those that cook more quickly. As they cook, move the vegetables up the sides of the wok to make space in the center for the next addition, or remove them and return them to the wok to reheat with the meat. Always keep the heat at maximum, and be careful not to put too much food in the wok at one time or the temperature will drop and your food will be soggy instead of crispy.

- To finish the dish, return the meat to the wok, add the sauce (bring it to a boil if it contains cornstarch) and serve immediately.

A Note About the Mortar and Pestle

This is a key piece of equipment in Thai cuisine and no Thai kitchen is complete without it. They are usually made of granite or heavy ceramic and come in many sizes. Many Thai recipes start with pounding together a spice paste that is the foundation of the dish. This gives the food the multi-layered taste and aroma that characterizes Thai food. It is possible to use a food processor to grind a spice paste, but then you are actually slicing the ingredients with the blade rather than pounding them together. This will result in a usable spice paste, but the flavor will not be the same as paste made using the traditional method.

Curry Pastes, Sauces and Broths

Red Curry Paste

15	dried hot chili peppers	15
1	2-inch (5-cm) cube fresh galanga root	1
2	stalks lemon grass	2
2 Tbsp.	coriander seeds	30 mL
2 Tbsp.	cumin seeds	30 mL
4 tsp.	paprika	20 mL
1/4 tsp.	turmeric	1.2 mL
1/4 tsp.	cinnamon	1.2 mL
3	1/2-inch (1.2-cm) pieces lime rind, finely chopped	3
6	shallots (or 1/2 onion), chopped	6
5	cilantro roots, cleaned and diced (or 10 stems)	5
6	cloves garlic, chopped	6
1 1/2 tsp.	shrimp paste	7.5 mL
	pinch salt	
1/2	red bell pepper, diced	1/2

Red curry paste is considered to be the all-purpose curry paste in Thai cuisine. It is appropriate for use in meat, poultry, seafood and vegetable curries and is a great flavor enhancer for soups and stir-fries. I have added red bell pepper to the recipe as a way of cutting back on the chilies. If you want a hotter or milder version of this paste, adjust the chilies or bell pepper accordingly.

Remove and discard the seeds from the chili peppers (if you want a milder paste). Cover with warm water and soak for 30 minutes.

Peel and chop the galanga. Finely slice the lemon grass, discarding the top and root.

Roast the coriander and cumin together in a dry frying pan over medium heat until a little smoke rises from the seeds (a few minutes). Grind in a mortar and pestle, then add the paprika, turmeric and cinnamon.

Drain the chilies, saving the liquid. Purée the chilies with all the other ingredients in a blender or processor until a fine paste is achieved. The texture should be similar to soft peanut butter. Use the chili water to thin the paste if necessary.

Makes about 1 cup (240 mL).

Green Curry Paste

Green curry paste is usually used to make chicken, seafood (Monkfish in Green Coconut Curry Sauce, page 75), pork or vegetarian curry. The difference in flavor between red and green curry paste can be compared to the difference in flavor between red and green bell peppers.

Roast the coriander and cumin seeds in a dry frying pan on medium heat until fragrant, about 3 minutes. Pound the seeds in a mortar and pestle or grind in a small electric coffee grinder.

Place the seeds and all the remaining ingredients in a blender or processor and purée to a fine paste.

Makes about $^3/_4$ cup (180 mL).

2 Tbsp.	coriander seeds	30 mL
2 Tbsp.	cumin seeds	30 mL
10	small green chilies	10
2	stalks lemon grass, sliced, top and root removed	2
1 Tbsp.	chopped lime peel	15 mL
1	2-inch (5-cm) cube galanga root	1
5 Tbsp.	chopped cilantro stems	75 mL
4	cloves garlic	4
5	shallots (or 1/2 onion), sliced	5
2 tsp.	shrimp paste	10 mL
1	small green bell pepper, sliced	1

Freezing Curry Paste

Curry paste will keep for a month when refrigerated. It will keep in the freezer for at least three months. I like to make a large amount and divide it into resealable plastic bags. Place the bags flat on a baking sheet to freeze them; when they are hard you can stack them in the freezer. When you need a small quantity for a sauce, you can break off a chunk and reseal the bag.

Panaeng Curry Paste

2 Tbsp.	coriander seeds	30 mL
2 Tbsp.	cumin seeds	30 mL
10	dried small red chilies, chopped	10
1	small onion, diced	1
4	large cloves garlic	4
2	stalks lemon grass, top and root removed, chopped	2
3 Tbsp.	chopped galanga	45 mL
3 Tbsp.	chopped cilantro stems	45 mL
1/4 cup	chopped, roasted unsalted peanuts	60 ml
1 tsp.	shrimp paste	5 mL

This curry paste is from the north of Thailand. The roasted peanuts give it a very rich flavor. It is usually used to make beef curry.

Roast the coriander and cumin seeds in a dry frying pan until fragrant. Pound them in a mortar and pestle or grind in a small electric coffee grinder.

Pound or blend the seeds and the remaining ingredients to make a smooth paste.

Makes $1/2$ cup (120 mL).

Massaman Curry Paste

This curry paste originated in southern Thailand and is usually used in chicken and beef curries. The influence from Malaysia can be seen in the use of fragrant spices such as cardamom, nutmeg and cloves. Massaman is said to be a corruption of the words "Muslim man," a reference to the most prevalent religion in Malaysia.

Heat the oil in a frying pan or wok over medium heat. Add the onion and garlic and fry until golden brown. Add the chilies and cook for 2 more minutes, stirring constantly.

Purée the onion, garlic and chili mixture in a food processor or blender together with the remaining ingredients. Alternatively, use a mortar and pestle to pound the spices, then mash the spices with the remaining ingredients to form a paste.

Makes about 1 1/2 cups (360 mL).

2 tsp.	vegetable oil	10 mL
1/2 cup	sliced onion	120 mL
1/2 cup	cloves garlic	120 mL
8	whole dry red chilies	8
1/4 cup	chopped lemon grass	60 mL
1	2-inch (5-cm) cube galanga root	1
1/2 tsp.	lime zest	2.5 mL
1 Tbsp.	coriander seeds	15 mL
2 Tbsp.	cumin seeds	30 mL
1 tsp.	nutmeg	5 mL
1/2 tsp.	cinnamon	2.5 mL
1/2 tsp.	cloves	2.5 mL
3	cardamom pods	3
1 Tbsp.	shrimp paste	15 mL

Roasted Chili Paste

¹/₄ cup	oil	60 mL
3 Tbsp.	chopped garlic	45 mL
3 Tbsp.	chopped shallots	45 mL
3	large dried red chilies, seeded and coarsely chopped	3
2 Tbsp.	sugar	30 mL
1 tsp.	salt	5 mL

This chili paste—called *Nam Prig Pow*—has a very rich smoky flavor because of the caramelizing of the garlic, chilies and shallots. It is ideal for adding flavor and heat to soups and stir-fries.

Heat the oil in a saucepan over medium heat and fry the garlic, stirring constantly, until golden brown. Remove with a slotted spoon and set aside. In the same oil, fry the shallots until crispy and golden brown; remove and set aside. Fry the chilies until they darken slightly; remove from the pan.

Place the chilies, shallot and garlic in a mortar or food processor. Pound with a pestle or process to a paste. Reheat the oil, add the paste and warm through. Add the sugar and salt and mix well to produce a thick, black-red sauce. This paste will keep for several weeks in the fridge and can be frozen for 3 months.

Makes ¹/₂ cup (120 mL).

Creamy Peanut Sauce

Peanut sauce can be found all over Thailand and there are literally hundreds of variations. It is usually served as a condiment with satays or spring rolls. The recipes here are four of my favorites. *Note:* When using peanut butter it is essential that the temperature never reaches the boiling point or the peanut butter will separate.

2 tsp.	oil	10 mL
1/4 cup	onion, finely diced	60 mL
1 1/2 tsp.	garlic, finely diced	7.5 mL
1 1/2 tsp.	minced fresh ginger	7.5 mL
3/4 cup	coconut milk	180 mL
1 tsp.	Red Curry Paste (page 8), or hot sauce	5 mL
1 1/2 Tbsp.	palm or brown sugar	22.5 mL
1 Tbsp.	fish sauce	15 mL
1/2 cup	chunky peanut butter	120 mL
2 Tbsp.	chopped cilantro	30 mL

Place the oil in a saucepan over high heat and sauté the onion, garlic and ginger until soft, about 1 minute.

Add the coconut milk, curry paste, brown sugar and fish sauce. Simmer on medium heat until the coconut milk is warm.

Turn off the heat and whisk in the peanut butter until it is melted. Stir in the cilantro.

Makes about 1 1/2 cups (360 mL).

Pineapple Peanut Sauce

¹/₂ cup	chicken stock	120 mL
¹/₂ cup	pineapple, minced	120 mL
¹/₂ cup	pineapple juice	120 mL
¹/₂ tsp.	curry powder	2.5 mL
1 Tbsp.	fish sauce	15 mL
1 Tbsp.	palm or brown sugar	15 mL
1 tsp.	crushed chilies	5 mL
2	cloves garlic, crushed	2
3 Tbsp.	chunky-style peanut butter	45 ml

This sauce goes particularly well with pork satay and is a great dipping sauce for sliced raw vegetables.

In a small saucepan, combine the stock, pineapple and juice, curry powder, fish sauce, brown sugar, chilies and garlic. Bring this mixture to a boil and simmer for a couple of minutes. Turn off the heat and whisk in the peanut butter.

Makes 1³/₄ cups (420 mL).

Thai Hoisin Peanut Sauce

The hoisin in this version of peanut sauce creates a complex, slightly sweet flavor that works well with chicken or pork satay.

1 Tbsp.	oil	15 mL
1/4 cup	onion, finely diced	60 mL
1 1/2 tsp.	minced fresh ginger	7.5 mL
1	clove garlic, diced	1
1 Tbsp.	fish sauce	15 mL
3/4 cup	chicken stock	180 mL
1 tsp.	Red Curry Paste (page 8)	5 mL
1 1/2 Tbsp.	hoisin sauce	22.5 mL
1/2	lime, juiced	1/2
1/2 cup	chunky peanut butter	120 mL
2 Tbsp.	chopped cilantro	30 mL

Heat the oil in a saucepan over high heat. Sauté the onion, ginger and garlic until soft, about 1 minute.

Add the fish sauce, chicken stock, curry paste, hoisin sauce and lime juice. Simmer on medium heat until the chicken stock is warm.

Turn off the heat and whisk in the peanut butter until it is melted. Stir in the cilantro.

Makes about 1 1/2 cups (360 mL).

Tamarind Peanut Sauce

1/2 cup	coconut milk	120 mL
1 Tbsp.	Red Curry Paste (page 8)	15 ml
2/3 cup	finely chopped roasted peanuts	160 ml
1/2 cup	chicken stock	120 mL
3 Tbsp.	palm or brown sugar	45 mL
2 Tbsp.	tamarind water (see page 48)	30 ml
1 Tbsp.	fish sauce	15 mL
1/2 tsp.	salt	2.5 mL

This sauce gets its sweet and sour flavor from the tartness of the tamarind. The roasted peanuts give it a crunchy texture. It is great with fish and seafood satays.

Heat the coconut milk in a pan until it comes to a boil. Stir in the curry paste until it's dissolved. Add the peanuts, stock and sugar and cook for about 5 minutes on medium heat. Turn the heat off and add the tamarind water, fish sauce and salt.

Makes 1 1/2 cups (360 mL).

Sweet Hot Tamarind Sauce

2 Tbsp.	oil	30 mL
1	small onion, diced	1
4	cloves garlic, finely diced	4
1 tsp.	Red Curry Paste (page 8)	5 ml
4	red chilies, thinly sliced	4
2 Tbsp.	chopped cilantro stems	30 mL
1/4 cup	palm or brown sugar	60 mL
1 cup	tamarind water (page 48)	240 ml
1 Tbsp.	soy sauce	15 mL

This sauce has a sweet and sour flavor that's great with spring rolls and with grilled fish or chicken.

Heat the oil in a saucepan over medium heat and fry the onion, garlic and curry paste together for 2 minutes. Add the chilies, cilantro, sugar, tamarind water and soy sauce and bring to a boil. Lower the heat to a simmer and cook for 10 minutes. This sauce will keep in the fridge for up to 3 days.

Makes about 1 1/2 cups (360 mL).

Coconut Ginger Sauce

This sauce has a creamy texture and a subtle flavor. It is ideal with salmon, but it's wonderful with any kind of seafood.

Heat the oil in a saucepan over high heat. Add the shallot and ginger and fry until they are soft and translucent. Add the coconut milk. Bring it almost to a boil and add the soy sauce, sugar, lime juice, zest and basil.

Makes about 1$\frac{1}{2}$ cups (360 mL).

1 Tbsp.	oil	15 mL
2 tsp.	chopped shallots	10 mL
2 tsp.	chopped fresh ginger	10 mL
1 cup	coconut milk	240 mL
2 Tbsp.	soy sauce	30 mL
2 Tbsp.	palm or brown sugar	30 mL
1 Tbsp.	lime juice	15 mL
1 tsp.	lime zest	5 mL
2 Tbsp.	chopped basil	30 mL

Honey Lime Sauce

This sauce is ideal with Spicy Cilantro Roast Chicken, page 101, but it is great with any roasted or barbecued chicken dish. It can also be used as a substitute for sweet chili sauce.

Bring all ingredients to a boil, then simmer for 20 minutes on low heat.

Makes 2 cups (475 mL).

1 cup	honey	240 mL
$\frac{1}{2}$ cup	water	120 mL
$\frac{1}{4}$ cup	lime juice	60 mL
$\frac{1}{4}$ cup	rice vinegar	60 mL
2 Tbsp.	minced garlic	30 mL
1 Tbsp.	chili paste or hot sauce	15 mL

Yellow Curry Sauce

1 cup	chicken or vegetable stock	240 ml
1	small onion	1
2 Tbsp.	chopped galanga	30 mL
3	cloves garlic	3
2 tsp.	ground turmeric	10 mL
2 tsp.	ground cumin	10 mL
1 tsp.	ground coriander	5 mL
1 Tbsp.	shrimp paste	15 mL
1 tsp.	salt	5 mL
5	small green chilies	5
2 cups	coconut milk	475 mL
2 tsp.	palm or brown sugar	10 mL
3 Tbsp.	fish sauce	45 mL

This is one of the two sauces used for *Knom Jeen* (page 45) and it also makes a tasty sauce to cook vegetables in.

Place the stock in a blender. Add the onion, galanga, garlic, turmeric, cumin, coriander, shrimp paste, salt and chilies. Purée till smooth.

Pour this mixture into a pan and bring to a boil. Add the coconut milk, sugar and fish sauce and return to a boil. Simmer for 5 minutes.

Makes about 3 cups (720 mL).

Nam Pla Prig

¹/₂ cup	fish sauce	120 mL
¹/₄ cup	water	60 mL
3 Tbsp.	sliced small red or green chilies	45 ml
¹/₂ tsp.	white sugar	2.5 mL

The name of this sauce literally means chili fish water. It is a condiment meant to be drizzled over food at the table to add heat (the chili) and salt (the fish sauce).

Stir together until the sugar is dissolved.

Makes ³/₄ cup (180 mL).

Dipping Sauce for Dumplings

This simple mixture is commonly used with pan-fried dumplings or potstickers. The vinegar is felt to cut the oil flavor from the frying. I sometimes add a little chopped shallot and cilantro to this sauce.

6 Tbsp.	soy sauce	90 mL
2 Tbsp.	Chinese red vinegar or balsamic vinegar	30 ml
2 tsp.	sugar	10 mL
2 tsp.	sesame oil	10 mL

Stir together and serve.

Makes about $^1/_2$ cup (120 mL).

Apricot Ginger Dipping Sauce

$^1/_2$ cup	apricot jam	120 mL
$1^1/_2$ tsp.	rice vinegar	7.5 mL
1 Tbsp.	chopped fresh ginger	15 mL
1 Tbsp.	soy sauce	15 mL

This is a great sauce with spring rolls and a tasty condiment with any poultry dish.

Stir all the ingredients together and thin with water to the desired consistency.

Makes about $^3/_4$ cup (180 mL).

Green Peppercorn Dip

$^1/_4$ cup	green peppercorns (bottled or canned)	60 ml
4	cloves garlic	4
2 tsp.	palm or brown sugar	5 mL
1 Tbsp.	dried shrimp, finely chopped	15 ml
$^1/_4$ cup	lime juice	60 mL

This spicy dip is great as a low-fat condiment for grilled fish. It can also be served as a dip with thinly sliced green mango or tart green apples.

In a mortar and pestle, pound the peppercorns, garlic and sugar together. Add the shrimp and lime juice and continue pounding until well combined.

Makes about $^3/_4$ cup (180 mL).

Quick Sweet and Sour Chili Sauce

This sauce can be made in under 15 minutes and will keep in the fridge for 10 days. It is commonly used with grilled or barbecued chicken and is the perfect accompaniment for Sweet Corn Patties, page 32.

1 cup	rice vinegar	240 mL
$^1/_2$ cup	palm or brown sugar	120 mL
3	cloves garlic, crushed	3
2	hot red chilies, minced	2
1 tsp.	salt	5 mL

Bring all the ingredients to a boil and simmer until it thickens, about 10 minutes.

Makes about 1$^1/_2$ cups (360 mL).

Sweet Chili Sauce

4 tsp.	oil	20 mL
1	medium onion, diced	1
8	cloves garlic, diced	8
2	fresh red chilies, diced, or dried chilies, soaked and diced	2
1	red bell pepper, diced	1
1/3 cup	palm or brown sugar	80 mL
2 Tbsp.	fish sauce	30 mL
2 Tbsp.	rice vinegar	30 mL
1 cup	water	240 mL
1 cup	chicken or vegetable stock	240 mL

This sauce is usually served with barbecued chicken in the north of Thailand, but it makes a great dipping sauce for corn patties or spring rolls.

Heat 2 tsp. (10 mL) of the oil in a saucepan over medium heat, and sauté the onion, garlic, chilies and red pepper until lightly browned.

Place $^2/_3$ of the sautéed mixture in a blender, add the sugar, fish sauce and vinegar and purée until smooth.

Heat the remaining 2 tsp. (10 mL) of oil over high heat. Return the puréed mixture to the pan with the remaining sautéed vegetables, and sauté the mixture for a couple of minutes. Add the water or stock, then bring to a boil. Cool before using.

Note: The taste can be varied by adding more water, or extra sugar or chilies. To make a thicker sauce, mix together 1 Tbsp. (15 mL) cornstarch and 3 Tbsp. (45 mL) cold water. Stir it into the sauce and bring to a boil.

Makes $2^1/_2$ cups (600 mL).

Ginger Cream Sauce

This sauce has a very mild ginger flavor that is perfect with prawns, scallops or chicken.

Heat the butter and oil in a saucepan over high heat. Add the shallots and garlic and sauté for 2 minutes. Add the ginger and sauté, stirring, for 2 minutes.

Add the wine, fish sauce and white pepper. Bring to a boil, then reduce the heat to medium and cook, stirring, for 3 minutes.

Add the coconut milk and cream. Increase the heat to high and bring to a boil. Reduce the heat to low and simmer until it is reduced by half, about 5 minutes. Strain the sauce through a fine sieve and keep warm until serving time.

Makes about 1 cup (240 mL).

2 Tbsp.	butter	30 mL
2 Tbsp.	olive oil	30 mL
2 Tbsp.	chopped shallots	30 mL
2 Tbsp.	chopped garlic	30 mL
1/4 cup	finely chopped, peeled fresh ginger	60 ml
1/2 cup	dry white wine	120 mL
1 Tbsp.	fish sauce	15 mL
2 tsp.	ground white pepper	10 mL
3/4 cup	coconut milk	180 mL
1 1/4 cups	whipping cream	300 mL

Smoked Oyster Coconut Sauce

1/2	onion, chopped	1/2
2	stalks lemon grass, finely chopped	2
1 Tbsp.	shrimp paste	15 mL
1 Tbsp.	Red Curry Paste (page 8)	15 mL
1 cup	smoked oysters, chopped	240 mL
2 cups	coconut milk	475 mL
1 tsp.	palm or brown sugar	5 mL
1 Tbsp.	fish sauce	15 mL

This sauce derives a lot of flavor from the smoked oysters. It goes well with fish patties but can also be used with grilled fish. You can substitute smoked trout for the oysters.

In a mortar and pestle or blender, purée the onion, lemon grass, shrimp paste, curry paste and 1/2 cup (120 mL) of the smoked oysters.

Heat the coconut milk to boiling and add the paste.

Lower the heat to medium and simmer for 5 minutes. Add the remaining smoked oysters, the sugar and fish sauce and simmer for another 5 to 10 minutes. It will keep for 1 day in the fridge.

Makes about 2 1/2 cups (600 mL).

Thai Chicken Stock

Any soup or sauce that you make will only taste as good as the stock that you make it from. This stock will add a subtle Thai flavor to your cooking. Homemade stock has infinitely more flavor than bouillon cubes and is easier to make than most people think. Chicken backs or necks (no skin) could be used or even the bones from roast chicken. Chicken stock can be divided into containers and frozen for months. If you freeze it in ice-cube trays, it's easy to add a little bit to a stir-fry or sauce. Remember—for a clear stock, do not stir it while it is simmering.

3 lbs.	chicken bones	1.4 kg
1	large onion, diced	1
2	ribs celery, diced	2
4	stalks lemon grass, cut in 2-inch (5-cm) pieces	4
6	kaffir lime leaves	6
1 tsp.	coriander seeds	5 mL
1 tsp.	whole black peppercorns	5 mL
1/4 cup	chopped fresh ginger	60 mL

Place the bones in a stockpot and cover with 4 inches (10 cm) water. Bring to a boil and skim off the gray foam that rises to the top. Add all the other ingredients and lower the heat to a simmer.

Simmer for 4 hours (add some water if the liquid drops below the level of the bones), then strain through cheesecloth or a fine sieve.

Makes about 16 cups (4 L).

Lemon Grass Broth

4 cups	chicken or vegetable stock	950 ml
2 cups	chopped lemon grass	475 mL
2 Tbsp.	chopped fresh ginger	30 mL
4	cloves garlic, coarsely chopped	4
1	sliced onion	1
3 Tbsp.	chopped cilantro stems	45 mL
2	kaffir lime leaves	2
2 Tbsp.	lime juice	30 mL
1 tsp.	salt	5 mL
1	small chili	1
1 tsp.	sugar	5 mL
1 tsp.	soy sauce	5 mL

I use this broth for poaching chicken or fish and as a cooking liquid for vegetables. It is great for low-fat cooking and infuses a subtle flavor that does not overwhelm the natural taste of the poached item.

Bring all ingredients, except the sugar and soy sauce, to a boil. Lower the heat and simmer until it's reduced by half, about 30 minutes.

Strain the broth and stir in the sugar and soy sauce.

Makes about 2 cups (475 mL).

Appetizers

Minced Chicken and Water Chestnut Dumplings

For the filling:

2 tsp.	oil	10 mL
1	onion, diced	1
1 tsp.	chopped fresh ginger	5 mL
1	clove garlic, chopped	1
8 oz.	ground chicken (or turkey or pork)	227 g
1/2 cup	chopped water chestnuts	120 mL
1 tsp.	salt	5 mL
1 tsp.	fish sauce	5 mL
1/4 cup	chopped cilantro	60 mL
1/2 cup	chopped roasted peanuts	120 mL

For the dough:

1/4 cup	tapioca flour	60 mL
2 cups	rice flour	475 mL
1/4 cup	coconut milk	60 mL
2 Tbsp.	oil	30 mL
1/4 cup	water	60 mL

For the sauce:

1 cup	coconut milk	240 mL
1 tsp.	turmeric	5 mL
1 tsp.	soy sauce	5 mL

For the garnish:

1/4 cup	crispy fried garlic	60 mL

This dumpling is similar to a Chinese dim sum item called *fun kor*. It is a little labor-intensive but definitely worth the effort. Serve it with Dipping Sauce for Dumplings (page 19) for a low-fat snack.

To make the filling, heat the oil to medium-hot in a saucepan. Add the onion, ginger and garlic and stir-fry until the onion is soft and translucent.

Add the ground meat, water chestnuts, salt and fish sauce. Cook until the meat is no longer pink. Add the cilantro and peanuts and set aside to cool.

To make the dough, mix the tapioca flour, rice flour, coconut milk, oil and water together in a saucepan. Add a little more water, if needed, to form a ball of dough. Cook over low heat, stirring constantly, until the mixture turns into an elastic dough. Remove from the heat, cover with plastic wrap and let the dough rest for 10 minutes.

Pinch off a small ball of dough and flatten with your finger into a 2 1/2-inch (6-cm) circle. Place a small spoonful of the filling on the circle. Pull the edges of the dough up and around the filling and pinch it closed with your fingers. You should have about 16 dumplings. Place in a steamer basket lined with an oiled banana leaf or lettuce leaf. Steam for 5 to 8 minutes.

To make the sauce, bring the coconut milk, turmeric and soy sauce to a boil while the dumplings are steaming. Spoon a bit over each dumpling and sprinkle a bit of crispy garlic on top.

Serves 4 as a snack.

Khanom Krok Coconut Dumplings

These sweet little dumplings are a breakfast snack sold by street vendors. They are made in a skillet designed for this dish—a heavy, cast-iron pan with six or eight round indentations in the bottom about the size of a golf ball cut in half. If you cannot find the right pan, you could make these in the oven in a muffin pan.

For the bottom layer:

1 cup	rice flour	240 mL
1 Tbsp.	all-purpose flour	15 mL
1 Tbsp.	tapioca starch	15 mL
1/2 tsp.	salt	2.5 mL
1 1/2 cups	coconut milk	360 mL
1/4 cup	water	60 mL

For the top layer:

1 cup	coconut milk	240 mL
1 tsp.	salt	5 mL
1/2 cup	white sugar	120 mL

To prepare the bottom layer, whisk together the rice flour, flour, tapioca starch, salt, coconut milk and water.

To prepare the top layer, in a separate bowl whisk together the 1 cup (240 mL) coconut milk, 1 tsp. (5 mL) salt and sugar.

To make the dumplings, heat the pan until hot. Oil the indentations in the pan with a brush. Pour 2 Tbsp. (30 mL) of the bottom layer mixture into each oiled indentation. Pour 1 tsp. (5 mL) of the top layer mixture over it.

Reduce the heat to medium, cover and cook for about 3 minutes, or until the edges turn brown.

If you are using a muffin pan, preheat the oven to 350°F (175°C). Oil the muffin cups and fill with the batter and topping, as above. Bake for about 15 minutes, or until the edges turn brown.

Lift out carefully with a spoon and serve immediately. Garnish with toasted shredded coconut or chopped green onion, if you like.

Serves 4 as a breakfast snack or an appetizer.

Duck and Mushroom Potstickers with Apricot Ginger Dipping Sauce

1/2 tsp.	black peppercorns	2.5 mL
1 tsp.	chopped fresh ginger	5 mL
2 Tbsp.	cilantro stems	30 mL
3 Tbsp.	oil	45 mL
1	onion, finely diced	1
2	cloves garlic, chopped	2
1 cup	finely diced mushrooms	240 mL
1 cup	diced Lime and Honey Roasted Duck (page 90)	240 mL
1 cup	finely diced water chestnuts	240 mL
1 Tbsp.	flour	15 mL
2 Tbsp.	soy sauce	30 mL
1 tsp.	sugar	5 mL
24	gyoza or won ton wrappers	24
1 recipe	Apricot Ginger Dipping Sauce (page 20)	1 recipe

These potstickers can be made with purchased Chinese barbecued duck, which eliminates one step in the preparation. Roasted chicken is another possible substitution, but the duck and apricot are a particularly delicious combination. Remember it is essential to have the skillet hot before cooking the potstickers, otherwise they really will stick. These dumplings can be stored in the fridge for several hours before cooking, but they have to be stored on a plate heavily dusted with cornstarch or else they will get soggy and stick to the plate.

In a mortar and pestle, crush the peppercorns. Add the ginger and cilantro and pound into a paste. Set aside.

Heat 1 Tbsp. (15 mL) of the oil in a skillet and fry the onion, garlic and mushrooms over high heat for 2 minutes. Set aside to cool.

In a bowl, combine the duck, water chestnuts, the cilantro paste, flour, soy sauce, sugar and the mushroom mixture.

Lay the wrappers on your work surface and place 1 Tbsp. (15 mL) filling in the center of each wrapper. Dip your finger in water and moisten the edge of each wrapper. Fold the wrapper over the filling and pinch the edges to seal.

Heat the remaining 2 Tbsp. (30 mL) oil in a heavy 12-inch (30-cm) skillet over high heat. When the oil is very hot, add the dumplings and cook until golden brown on the bottom. Add 1 cup (240 mL) water to the skillet, cover and cook until the water is absorbed (a few minutes). (Or steam in a basket for 5 minutes.) Serve with Apricot Ginger Dipping Sauce.

Makes about 2 dozen potstickers.

Spinach and Mushroom Potstickers

These little dumplings are so tasty I sometimes have them for a whole meal. It is essential to have the pan and oil hot before frying them, otherwise they will stick. Don't be tempted to use too much filling or they will open up during cooking. There are infinite possibilities for fillings, so once you have perfected the technique for filling and frying the potstickers, try some different fillings. You could add cooked chopped chicken or substitute uncooked fish cake mixture (page 33). If gyoza wrappers are not available, use won ton wrappers; they are a little thinner and you will not get the half-moon shape, but they will taste good.

15	black peppercorns	15
2 Tbsp.	cilantro stems	30 mL
3 Tbsp.	oil	45 mL
1	onion, finely diced	1
2	cloves garlic, chopped	2
1 cup	finely diced mushrooms	240 mL
1 cup	finely diced bamboo shoots	240 ml
1 cup	chopped, blanched spinach	240 mL
1 cup	finely diced water chestnuts	240 ml
1 Tbsp.	flour	15 mL
2 Tbsp.	soy sauce	30 mL
1 tsp.	sugar	5 mL
1 tsp.	chopped fresh ginger	5 mL
1 package	round won ton or gyoza wrappers	1 package

In a mortar and pestle, pound the peppercorns and cilantro into a paste. Set aside.

Heat 1 Tbsp. (15 mL) of the oil in a pan over medium heat. Add the onion, garlic and mushrooms and fry until the onions are soft. Place the bamboo shoots, spinach, water chestnuts, cilantro paste, flour, soy sauce, sugar, ginger and the mushroom mixture in a bowl and mix thoroughly.

Lay the wrappers on your work surface and place 1 Tbsp. (15 mL) filling in the center of each wrapper. Dip your finger in water and moisten the edge of each wrapper. Fold the wrapper over the filling and pinch the edges to seal.

Heat the remaining 2 Tbsp. (30 mL) oil in a heavy 12-inch (30-cm) skillet over high heat. When the oil is very hot, add the dumplings and cook until golden brown on the bottom. Add 1 cup (240 mL) of water to the skillet, and cover immediately. Cook until the water is absorbed, a few minutes. (Or steam them in a basket for 5 minutes.)

Serve with Dipping Sauce for Dumplings (page 19).

Makes about 2 dozen.

Sweet Corn Patties

2 tsp.	Szechuan peppercorns	10 mL
2 cups	corn kernels (fresh, or frozen and defrosted)	475 ml
1 tsp.	fish sauce or soy sauce	5 mL
2 tsp.	minced garlic	10 mL
2 Tbsp.	flour	30 mL
2	eggs	2
1/4 cup	chopped cilantro	60 mL
1 lb.	minced prawns, chicken or pork (optional)	455 g
2 Tbsp.	oil	30 mL

Corn patties are the type of item you would see for sale as a snack on the streets of Bangkok. There are dozens of variations: some are pan-fried; some are deep-fried like fritters. Adding the minced prawns or meat makes them firmer and easier to turn over in the pan. The Szechuan peppercorns give these patties an exotic aroma—fragrant, rather than hot. It is essential to start with a hot skillet, otherwise they will stick to the pan. When you put the batter in the pan, wait a minute or two before attempting to move the patties; this will also help prevent them from sticking.

Toast the Szechuan peppercorns in a dry frying pan over medium heat, stirring constantly, for about 5 minutes, or until they release their fragrance. Crush them in a mortar and pestle.

Purée 1/2 cup (120 mL) of the corn in a blender with a few spoonfuls of water. Combine the puréed corn with the fish or soy sauce, garlic, flour, eggs, cilantro, crushed pepper and minced meat, if desired. Mix to form a thick batter.

Heat the oil in a skillet until very hot and drop one large spoonful at a time into the hot pan. Lower the heat to medium and fry until golden brown on one side; turn them over and brown the other side.

Serve with Sweet Chili Sauce (page 22).

Serves 4 to 6.

Fish and Vegetable Patties

These fish patties are a very traditional and popular appetizer, so, as usual, you will find many different versions. Experiment with different combinations of fish (you could even add prawns or scallops) for a variety of flavors.

Purée the green pepper, chilies, garlic, lemon grass and fish sauce in a food processor. Add the fish fillets and purée into a paste.

Add the egg and coconut milk and pulse to combine.

Place the mixture in a bowl and stir in the green beans. Refrigerate overnight or at least 2 hours. (This helps to firm the batter.)

Heat the oil in a frying pan over high heat. Shape the fish mixture into small patties with the help of a spoon. Lower the heat to medium and fry until crisp and golden on both sides.

Serve with Sweet Chili Sauce (page 22) and Cucumber Chili Salad (page 69).

Makes about 24 patties.

1	green bell pepper, chopped	1
2	small red chilies	2
2	cloves garlic, chopped	2
1	stalk lemon grass, top and root removed, finely chopped	1
1 Tbsp.	fish sauce	15 mL
1 lb.	fish fillets (cod, snapper, etc.)	455 g
2	egg whites	2
1/2 cup	coconut milk	120 mL
1/2 cup	green beans, sliced into thin pieces, 1/8 inch (.3 cm)	120 ml
2 Tbsp.	oil	30 mL

Yam and Sesame Patties

1 lb.	yams	455 g
1/2 lb.	potatoes	227 g
2 Tbsp.	cilantro stems, chopped	30 mL
2 Tbsp.	cilantro leaves, chopped	30 mL
1/2 cup	dried, shredded unsweetened coconut	120 ml
1/2 cup	flour	120 mL
1 Tbsp.	sesame oil	15 mL
	salt and black pepper to taste	
1/2 cup	sesame seeds	120 mL
2 Tbsp.	oil	30 mL

There are numerous varieties of sweet potatoes and yams in Southeast Asia. This street snack is made with whatever type is at hand.

Cube the yams and potatoes. Place them in a saucepan, cover with water and add the cilantro stems.

Bring to a boil and cook until tender when pierced with a fork, about 15 minutes. Drain and return to the heat for a couple of minutes to dry. Mash and allow to cool slightly. Stir in the cilantro leaves, coconut, flour and sesame oil. Season with salt and pepper.

Dust your hands with flour and form the mixture into small patties. You should have about 20 patties. Dip them in sesame seeds. Heat the oil over medium-high in a skillet and fry the patties on both sides until lightly browned, about 5 minutes.

Makes 20 to 24 patties.

Spicy Street Satay

Satays are sold all over the streets of Southeast Asia. This results in as many versions as there are cooks, so don't be afraid to change the ingredients or use different proportions.

Cut the meat into thin strips about 1 x 3 inches (2.5 x 7.5 cm) long. Combine all remaining ingredients in a bowl. Toss the meat in the marinade and refrigerate for 1 to 2 hours.

Presoak 12 bamboo skewers in cold water for 30 minutes. Thread the meat onto the skewers and grill or broil over high heat on both sides for a total of 4 to 6 minutes.

Serve with peanut sauce (pages 13 to 16).

Serves 4.

1 lb.	chicken, beef or pork	455 g
1 tsp.	chopped garlic	5 mL
1 tsp.	fish sauce	5 mL
1 tsp.	palm or brown sugar	5 mL
1/2 tsp.	ground cumin	2.5 mL
1/2 tsp.	ground coriander	2.5 mL
1/2 tsp.	curry powder	2.5 mL
2 tsp.	Panaeng Curry Paste (page 10)	10 ml
1/4 cup	chicken stock	60 mL
1/4 cup	coconut milk	60 mL

Pork Satay

1 lb.	pork loin	455 g
1 tsp.	fish sauce	5 mL
1 tsp.	palm or brown sugar	5 mL
1/2 tsp.	ground cumin	2.5 mL
1/2 tsp.	ground coriander	2.5 mL
1/2 tsp.	turmeric	2.5 mL
1 tsp.	Red Curry Paste (page 8)	5 mL
2 tsp.	curry powder	10 mL
1/2 cup	coconut milk	120 mL

The fruitiness of Pineapple Peanut Sauce (page 14) is particularly nice with the pork.

Cut the pork into thin strips about 1 x 3 inches long (2.5 x 7.5 cm). Combine the remaining ingredients in a bowl. Toss the pork in the marinade and refrigerate for 1 to 2 hours.

Presoak 12 bamboo skewers in cold water for 30 minutes. Thread the pork onto the skewers and grill over a hot barbecue for about 4 to 6 minutes, turning once.

Serve with peanut sauce (pages 13 to 16).

Serves 4 as an appetizer.

Coconut Marinated Chicken Satay

Every family in Thailand has a different version of chicken satay. Experiment with various proportions of these ingredients to create your own.

Cut the chicken into thin strips, about $^1/_2$-inch (1.2-cm) wide and 4 inches (10 cm) long. Place in a medium bowl or a plastic bag.

In another bowl, combine the coconut milk, garlic, curry paste, ginger, fish sauce and cilantro. Combine with the chicken strips. Cover and marinate in the refrigerator at least 30 minutes or overnight.

Presoak 12 bamboo skewers in cold water for 30 minutes. Weave the chicken strips onto the skewers.

Grill the chicken skewers over a hot barbecue for about 2 minutes on each side. Serve with peanut sauce (pages 13 to 16).

Serves 4.

Note: If you don't have a barbecue, cut the chicken into 1-inch (2.5-cm) cubes instead of strips. After marinating, place the chicken cubes on a baking sheet in an oven preheated to 425ºF (220ºC), and bake for 15 minutes.

1 lb.	skinless boneless chicken breasts	455 g
1 cup	coconut milk	240 mL
2	cloves garlic, crushed	2
1 tsp.	Red Curry Paste (page 8)	5 mL
1 Tbsp.	chopped fresh ginger	15 mL
1 Tbsp.	fish sauce	15 mL
$^1/_4$ cup	chopped cilantro	60 mL

Spinach and Peanut Dip

2 tsp.	oil	10 mL
1	large onion, diced	1
4	cloves garlic, finely diced	4
2 Tbsp.	Red Curry Paste (page 8)	30 mL
1	14-oz. (398-mL) can coconut milk	1
1 cup	chicken or vegetable stock	240 mL
1/4 cup	fish sauce	60 mL
6 Tbsp.	palm or brown sugar	90 mL
2 cups	chopped roasted peanuts (unsalted)	475 mL
2	10-oz. (285-g) packages frozen chopped spinach (thawed)	2

Serve this dip with sliced raw vegetables, such as cucumber, carrots and celery. It also makes a great vegetable side dish. The recipe calls for frozen spinach for convenience, but of course you could use fresh spinach. The equivalent of one package of frozen spinach would be 4 bunches of fresh spinach, washed, trimmed, chopped and blanched.

Heat the oil in a skillet over high heat. When it's hot, add the onions and garlic and sauté until soft. Add the curry paste and sauté for 1 more minute.

Add the coconut milk, stock, fish sauce, sugar and peanuts. Continue to cook over medium heat, stirring constantly, for 10 minutes.

Add the spinach and stir until warm.

Makes about 4 cups (950 mL).

kaffir lime leaves

ginger

bananas

chilies

green mango

kaffir limes

tamarind pods

rice noodles

shallots

ripe mango

green papaya

galanga

Thai basil

lemon grass

Coconut Marinated Chicken Satay (page 37)

Khanom Krok Coconut Dumplings (page 29)

Leaf-wrapped Rice Noodles with Savories (page 45)

Thai Spring Rolls

There are hundreds of different fillings for spring rolls. Leftover stir-fry dishes make a good starting point for a filling—be bold and experiment! The real trick to making these is to not overfill them so they do not come apart when you fry them.

Mix the chicken, shrimp or pork with the fish sauce and sugar. Set aside.

Heat the 2 tsp. (10 mL) oil in a wok to very hot. Add the shallot, carrot and cabbage and stir-fry for 30 seconds.

Add the meat, bean sprouts and noodles and cook on high for another minute. Stir in the cilantro and set this mixture aside to cool.

Separate the spring roll wrappers and cover them with a damp cloth. Mix the water and flour together. To form the rolls, place a couple of spoonfuls of the filling mixture in the center of a wrapper. Fold the lower end of the wrapper over to cover the filling and roll it once to form the filling into a log shape. Fold in the 2 sides and continue rolling it up towards the end. Moisten the end with a little of the water-flour mixture and press to seal the spring roll.

Repeat until the filling is used up. Try to make the spring rolls all the same size so they will cook at the same rate.

Heat the 3 cups (720 mL) oil to 360°F (180°C). Place the spring rolls in the hot oil and fry until golden brown.

Serve with Sweet Chili Sauce, page 22.

Makes 24 small rolls.

4 oz.	skinless boneless chicken, shrimp or pork, diced	113 g
1 Tbsp.	fish sauce	30 mL
1 tsp.	sugar	5 mL
2 tsp.	oil	10 mL
1	shallot, diced	1
1	small carrot, grated	1
1 cup	shredded cabbage	240 mL
3 cups	mung bean sprouts	720 mL
1 oz.	rice noodles, soaked in warm water until soft and drained (see page 132)	30 g
1/4 cup	chopped cilantro	60 mL
24	small spring roll wrappers	24
1/2 cup	water	120 mL
3 Tbsp.	flour	45 mL
3 cups	oil, for frying	720 mL

Barbecued Duck and Mushroom
Fresh Spring Rolls

1 tsp.	sugar	5 mL
2 Tbsp.	soy sauce	30 mL
1 Tbsp.	sesame oil	15 mL
$^{1}/_{2}$ cup	chopped cilantro	120 mL
2 Tbsp.	chopped fresh ginger	30 mL
1 cup	blanched chopped spinach	240 mL
1 cup	sliced fried mushrooms	240 mL
1 cup	sliced Chinese-style barbecued duck	240 mL
1	long English cucumber	1
8	8-inch (20-cm) rice paper wraps	8
8	lettuce leaves	8
1	carrot, grated	1

These fresh spring rolls are one of my favorite appetizers. They can be made several hours before serving, if they are covered with a damp clean cloth and refrigerated. If barbecued duck is not available, barbecued chicken meat mixed with a little anise powder and a teaspoon (5 mL) of honey will give you a similar flavor.

Combine the sugar, soy sauce, sesame oil, cilantro and ginger in a bowl. Toss the spinach, fried mushrooms and barbecued duck in this mixture and set aside.

Cut 8 strips of cucumber that are 1 inch (2.5 cm) shorter than the rice wrappers.

Fill a wide shallow pan with hot water and spread a dish towel on a counter. Dip a wrapper in the water for about 10 seconds to soften it and place it on the towel.

Place a lettuce leaf on the rice wrapper. Place a strip of cucumber, $^{1}/_{8}$ of the spinach-duck mixture and $^{1}/_{8}$ of the carrot on the lettuce. Roll it up from the bottom, rolling it into a cylinder and tucking in the sides as you go.

Place the rolls, seam side down, on a platter covered with a damp cloth.

Serve with a peanut dipping sauce (pages 13 to 16).

Makes 8 spring rolls.

Northern Thai Whiskey-Marinated Chicken Wings

Thailand produces a pleasant-tasting spirit called Mekong whiskey. In Thailand it is easily available and less expensive than a bottle of beer. It gives a unique flavor to this chicken dish, although any type of whiskey or bourbon could be used as a substitute.

10	cloves garlic, finely diced	10
2 Tbsp.	palm or brown sugar	30 mL
3 Tbsp.	black peppercorns, crushed	45 mL
2 Tbsp.	soy sauce	30 mL
5 Tbsp.	whiskey or bourbon	75 mL
1 tsp.	salt	5 mL
2¹/₂ lbs.	chicken wings or drumettes	1.1 kg

Combine the garlic, sugar, peppercorns, soy sauce, whiskey and salt. Add the chicken wings and mix to coat with the marinade. Place in the fridge to marinate for 3 hours or overnight.

Preheat the oven to 375°F (190°C).

Place the wings on an oiled baking sheet and bake for 45 minutes, or until crisp.

Serve with Sweet Chili Sauce, page 22.

Serves 4 to 6.

Chicken Wings in Lemon Grass Red Wine Sauce

1 cup	red wine	240 mL
1/2 cup	tomato sauce	120 mL
3 Tbsp.	palm or brown sugar	45 mL
1 Tbsp.	chopped garlic	15 mL
1/4 cup	lemon grass, finely minced	60 mL
2	small red chilies, chopped	2
1/2 cup	diced onion	120 mL
1/4 cup	Maggi seasoning sauce	60 mL
1 Tbsp.	paprika	15 mL
1 lb.	chicken wings	455 g
2 tsp.	oil	10 mL
2 1/2 cups	water	600 mL

During my last trip to Thailand, my friend Brian took me for dinner at the Baan Muang (banana house) restaurant in Bangkok. I am always looking for new dishes, so when I spotted "chicken in red wine spoose" on the menu, I ordered it expecting to get chicken stuffed in an exotic vegetable I had never seen before. When it arrived I was somewhat disappointed to find out this was just one of the translation errors that are typical of menus in Southeast Asia. My disappointment faded quickly when I tasted the rich flavors in the sauce, and after much experimenting I think I have duplicated the taste of the "red wine spoose."

Combine the wine, tomato sauce, sugar, garlic, lemon grass, chilies, onion, Maggi seasoning sauce and paprika. Marinate the chicken wings in this mixture for at least 15 minutes or up to overnight in the fridge.

Heat the oil in a wok over high heat. Add the wing mixture and cook and stir for about 10 minutes. Add the water and boil for 3 minutes. Lower the heat and simmer for 30 minutes, or until the sauce thickens and coats the wings.

Serves 4.

Herbed and Sweetened Prawns

This dish is quite sweet and is meant to be eaten as a small appetizer. The best flavor is achieved by using prawns with the shell on. Prawn shells actually have more flavor than the meat. That is the reason for the intense flavor when they are used to make prawn stock or prawn bisque. If it is not possible to get the softer-shelled white prawns, use tiger prawns and snip open the shells on one side before cooking, so that it is easier to remove the shells when eating.

1 tsp.	Szechuan peppercorns	5 mL
3/4 cup	palm or brown sugar	180 mL
3 Tbsp.	fish sauce	45 mL
1/2 cup	water	120 mL
2 Tbsp.	chopped cilantro stems	30 mL
2	cloves garlic, crushed	2
2 cups	prawns, heads off, deveined, shells left on	475 mL

Toast the Szechuan peppercorns in a dry frying pan over medium heat, stirring constantly, for about 5 minutes, or until they release their fragrance. Crush them in a mortar and pestle.

Heat the sugar, fish sauce and water in a wok on high heat until the sugar is dissolved. Add the cilantro stems, garlic and peppercorns and continue cooking until the liquid is reduced by $1/3$.

Add the prawns and simmer over medium heat until the prawns are cooked and glazed in the caramelized sauce, about 4 minutes.

Soft-shelled white prawns will be tender enough to eat with the shells on; tiger prawns should be shelled.

Serves 4.

Lettuce Wraps

For the filling:

1 Tbsp.	oil	15 mL
1	onion, diced	1
1 lb.	ground beef, pork or chicken	455 g
1	egg, slightly beaten	1
1	carrot, grated	1
1 cup	finely sliced bamboo shoots	240 mL
1	green bell pepper, finely sliced	1
2	green chilies, seeded and diced	2
2 Tbsp.	soy sauce	30 mL
2 Tbsp.	sugar	30 mL

For the sauce:

1/4 cup	minced garlic	60 mL
1 Tbsp.	sugar	15 mL
1/2 cup	fish sauce	120 mL
1/3 cup	lime juice	80 mL
1 tsp.	chili oil or hot sauce	5 mL

For the wraps:

2	heads lettuce (iceberg or large greenleaf), separated into leaves	2
1 cup	chopped roasted peanuts	240 mL
1	cucumber, peeled and sliced	1
1 cup	shredded mint or basil leaves	240 mL

These are fun to serve at a buffet or to any group. People can make their own wraps, adding garnishes and sauce according to their taste. Any kind of ground meat or poultry will work. My favorite low-fat, low-cholesterol alternative to beef is ostrich; it tastes similar to beef but better.

To make the filling, heat the oil over medium-high, add the onion and meat and sauté for a few minutes, until the meat loses its pink color. Stir in the egg and continue stirring as it cooks. Add all the other filling ingredients and cook for another 1 to 2 minutes. Spoon into a serving dish.

To make the sauce, mix the sauce ingredients together in a bowl and set aside.

Arrange the lettuce leaves, peanuts, cucumber and shredded herbs on a platter.

To assemble, place a heaping spoonful of filling on a lettuce leaf. Add garnishes of choice and sauce to taste. Roll it up and eat it.

Serves 6.

Leaf-wrapped Rice Noodles with Savories

In Thai this dish is *knom jeen* and the literal translation is "Chinese snack." *Knom jeen* has many variations, as most Thai dishes do. This version is easier to prepare than some, which call for ingredients such as banana blossoms. I was first introduced to this afternoon snack by my friends Brian and Sanit. We went to visit Sanit's mother in Northern Thailand and she prepared this mini buffet on the veranda of her teak home. We sat on bamboo mats and feasted on these savory little packages with fresh rice noodles.

1 lb.	dried thin rice noodles	455 g
1	head lettuce or spinach, separated into leaves	1
2 cups	Yellow Curry Sauce (page 18)	475 mL
1 cup	Creamy Peanut Sauce (page 13)	240 mL
1 cup	thinly sliced cabbage	240 mL
1 cup	thinly sliced cucumber	240 mL
1 cup	bean sprouts	240 mL
1/2 cup	Thai basil, mint or cilantro	120 mL
1 Tbsp.	ground chilies	15 mL
1/2 cup	sliced fresh red chilies	120 mL
1/2 cup	shredded unsweetened coconut, toasted (see page 123)	120 mL
1 cup	sliced green onions	240 mL

Drop the rice noodles into a large pot of boiling water. Cook for 1 minute, or until softened. Drain and rinse under cold water (see page 132).

Place a small amount of the rice noodles on a lettuce leaf. Top with some curry sauce and a little peanut sauce. Scatter a little of the remaining ingredients over top before rolling the leaf up. Place seam-side down on a serving platter.

Another way of serving this is to set out all the ingredients in bowls, buffet-style, and have diners choose what they want to put in their lettuce wraps.

Serves 6.

Sanit's Sweet Chili Dip for Green Mango

1 Tbsp.	dried miniature crabs, or dried shrimp	15 mL
5	chopped shallots	5
4	cloves garlic, chopped	4
6	sliced cherry tomatoes	6
$^1/_3$ cup	palm or brown sugar	80 mL
1 Tbsp.	roasted, dried, crushed red chilies	15 mL
2 Tbsp.	fish sauce	30 mL
1	large green mango	1

My friend Sanit is a great natural cook. One afternoon, on the veranda of his mother's house in the countryside of Petchaboon, north of Bangkok, he whipped this up with a mortar and pestle. It is a version of a dish that is a popular snack sold by street vendors. If green mangos are not available, you can use a tart green apple.

In a mortar and pestle, pound the crab or shrimp into small pieces. Add the shallots and garlic and keep pounding until you have a coarse paste. Add the tomatoes, sugar, chilies and fish sauce and pound again, using the fish sauce to dissolve the sugar.

When everything is thoroughly combined, set the mixture aside and let the flavors develop for 30 minutes.

Peel the mango and slice it into thin, wide strips. Use the mango strips to scoop up little bits of the sweet chili dip.

Makes about $^3/_4$ cup (180 mL).

Soups

Thai Roasted Vegetable and Chicken Soup

3	1/2-inch (1.2-cm) slices galanga	3
1	stalk lemon grass, sliced	1
4	kaffir lime leaves	4
6	shallots, sliced	6
4	cloves garlic, sliced	4
4	red chilies	4
1	whole, skinless boneless chicken breast, sliced	1
10	mushrooms, thickly sliced	10
4 cups	chicken stock	950 mL
2 Tbsp.	fish sauce	30 mL
2 Tbsp.	tamarind water	30 mL
1/2 cup	roughly chopped parsley	120 mL

The unique flavor of this soup, called *Tom Klong*, comes from the charring of the aromatics, often done over an open fire. The foil method is a lot easier and will result in the same wonderful-tasting soup.

Wrap the galanga, lemon grass, lime leaves, shallots, garlic and chilies loosely in foil. Roast over a barbecue or broil in the oven until lightly charred.

Combine the roasted items and the chicken, mushrooms and stock in a saucepan. Bring to a boil and simmer until the chicken is cooked, about 5 minutes. Add the fish sauce and tamarind water.

Cook for another 5 minutes and add the parsley.

Serves 2 to 4.

How to Make Tamarind Water

Place 3 Tbsp. (45 mL) dried tamarind pulp in a bowl and add 1/2 cup (120 mL) hot water. Let it soak for about 20 minutes, stirring occasionally to break up the lumps. When the pulp is soft, strain it through a fine sieve, pressing on the pulp to extract all the liquid. Keep the liquid and discard the pulp.

Makes about 1/2 cup (120 mL).

Thai Shrimp and Jasmine Rice Soup

This is Thai comfort food. It is similar to Chinese congee (rice porridge) and is the kind of soup that would be served for breakfast. It is essential to use rice that is cooked, as the texture of the rice in the soup is meant to be very soft.

In a soup pot, heat the stock to boiling. Add the Maggi seasoning sauce, pepper, galanga and celery.

Add the shrimp, rice and fish sauce. Stir thoroughly to break up any lumps of shrimp. Bring to a boil and simmer for 10 minutes.

Heat the oil in a small frying pan over medium-high, add the garlic and fry until it's light brown.

Pour the soup into bowls and garnish with the garlic and cilantro leaves.

Serves 4.

2 cups	chicken stock	475 mL
1 Tbsp.	Maggi seasoning sauce	15 mL
1/4 tsp.	white pepper	1.2 mL
1 tsp.	finely minced galanga	5 mL
2	stalks celery, thinly sliced	2
8 oz.	minced raw shrimp	227 mL
1 1/2 cups	cooked jasmine rice	360 mL
2 Tbsp.	fish sauce	30 mL
1 tsp.	vegetable oil	5 mL
4	cloves garlic, sliced	4
1/4 cup	cilantro leaves	60 mL

Chicken and Coconut Milk Soup

3 cups	coconut milk	720 mL
5	slices galanga, $^1/_4$ inch (.6 cm) thick	5
2	stalks lemon grass, cut in 2-inch (5-cm) pieces	2
5	kaffir lime leaves	5
8 oz.	skinless boneless chicken breast, cut in 1-inch (2.5-cm) cubes	227 g
3 Tbsp.	fish sauce	45 mL
3 Tbsp.	lime juice	45 mL
1 Tbsp.	palm or brown sugar	15 mL
$^1/_2$ cup	sliced mushrooms	120 mL
$^1/_4$ cup	chopped cilantro	60 mL
5	red chilies, diced	5

This soup—*Tom Kah Gai*—has all the defining flavors of Thai cuisine. The lime leaves and chunks of lemon grass and galanga are left in the soup as a colorful garnish, but are not meant to be eaten. The first time I was in Thailand I tried, unsuccessfully, to eat these garnishes, much to the amusement of the other Thai diners.

Combine the coconut milk, galanga, lemon grass and lime leaves. Bring to a boil, lower the heat and simmer for at least 40 minutes.

Add the chicken, fish sauce, lime juice, sugar and mushrooms. Bring to a boil and simmer for about 5 minutes, until the chicken is cooked.

Garnish with the cilantro leaves and diced red chilies. For a spicier version, add the chilies with the chicken.

Serves 2 to 4.

Tom Yam Prawn Soup

Tom Yam (spicy fragrant soup) is the most famous soup in Thai cuisine. It has all the defining flavors of a traditional dish—lemon grass, chili, lime, kaffir lime leaf, galanga, garlic. But the real key to the flavor in this dish is the stock made from the prawn shells. Whenever I peel prawns I throw the shells into the freezer until I have enough to make a big batch of prawn stock. The more shells that go into the stock the better the stock will taste.

3/4 lb.	prawns in the shell	340 g
1 tsp.	oil	5 mL
3 cups	chicken or fish stock	720 mL
2 cups	water	475 mL
3	stalks lemon grass, cut in 1/2-inch (1.2-cm) slices	3
5	kaffir lime leaves	5
2	small red chili peppers, sliced	2
1	clove garlic, minced	1
1	1-inch (2.5-cm) piece galanga, sliced	1
1 cup	sliced mushrooms	240 mL
1/2	onion, thinly sliced	1/2
1	stalk celery, thinly sliced	1
1	red bell pepper, thinly sliced	1
2	limes, juiced	2
1 Tbsp.	fish sauce	15 mL
3	green onions, sliced	3
1/4 cup	cilantro leaves and stems, sliced	60 mL

Remove the shells from the prawns, saving the shells. Slice the prawns in half lengthwise and refrigerate.

In a large soup pot, heat the oil and sauté the prawn shells until pink. Add the stock, water, lemon grass, lime leaves, chili peppers, garlic and galanga. Bring to a boil. Lower the heat, cover and simmer for 60 minutes.

Strain the stock mixture and return it to the pot. Bring to a boil and add the mushrooms, onion, celery and red pepper. Reduce the heat and simmer for 2 minutes.

Add the prawns and simmer for another 2 minutes. Add the lime juice, fish sauce, green onion and cilantro just before serving.

Serves 6.

Tom Yam Chicken Soup

3 cups	double Thai Chicken Stock (page 25)	720 mL
2 cups	water	475 mL
3	stalks lemon grass, cut in $^1/_2$-inch (1.2-cm) slices	3
5	kaffir lime leaves	5
2	red chili peppers, sliced, or 1 Tbsp. (15 mL) Red Curry Paste (page 8)	2
1	clove garlic, minced	1
1	1-inch (2.5-cm) piece galanga, sliced	1
1 cup	sliced mushrooms	240 mL
$^1/_2$	onion, thinly sliced	$^1/_2$
1	stalk celery, thinly sliced	1
1	red bell pepper, thinly sliced	1
$^3/_4$ lb.	skinless boneless chicken, sliced	340 g
2	limes, juiced	2
1 Tbsp.	fish sauce	15 mL
3	green onions, sliced	3
$^1/_4$ cup	cilantro leaves and stems, chopped	60 mL

Tom Yam is usually made with prawns, but it can also be made with chicken. The essence of this soup is a very rich-tasting stock, which is why I use a double chicken stock. To make a double chicken stock, use chicken stock instead of water when making the Thai Chicken Stock; this intensifies the flavor.

In a soup pot, combine the stock, water, lemon grass, lime leaves, chili peppers or curry paste, garlic and galanga. Bring to a boil. Lower the heat, cover and simmer for 30 minutes.

Strain the stock mixture and return it to the pot. Bring it to a boil and add the mushrooms, onion, celery and red pepper. Reduce the heat and simmer for 2 minutes.

Add the chicken and simmer for another 5 minutes. Just before serving, add the lime juice, fish sauce, green onion and cilantro.

Serves 6.

Coriander Broth with Prawn and Pork Dumplings

The flavor of the cilantro is infused into the broth when the meatballs simmer in the soup. The meatballs should be very small and a uniform size so they cook quickly and at the same rate.

2 cups	cilantro	475 mL
7 oz.	ground pork or chicken	200 g
3–4 oz.	ground prawns	85–113 g
2 Tbsp.	soy sauce	30 mL
1 tsp.	salt	5 mL
4 cups	chicken stock	950 mL
	salt and black pepper to taste	

Set aside a dozen cilantro leaves for a garnish. Chop the remaining leaves and stems and combine with the pork or chicken, prawns, soy sauce and salt.

Form the meat mixture into small meatballs. Bring the stock to a boil and drop the meatballs into the stock. Boil for 1 or 2 minutes, then lower the heat and simmer for about 5 minutes. Adjust the seasoning with salt and pepper.

Scatter the reserved cilantro leaves over the soup before serving.

Serves 4.

Herbed Prawn and Vegetable Soup

5	shallots	5
1 tsp.	black peppercorns	5 mL
1 Tbsp.	chopped cilantro stems	15 mL
1 tsp.	salt	5 mL
$^1/_2$ cup	minced dried shrimp	120 mL
$^1/_2$ cup	minced fresh prawns	120 mL
5 cups	vegetable or chicken stock	1.2 L
$^1/_2$ cup	whole fresh prawns, shelled	120 mL
2 cups	assorted sliced vegetables (baby corn, green beans, mushrooms, zucchini, etc.)	475 mL
2 Tbsp.	fish sauce	30 mL
1 tsp.	lime juice	5 mL
1 Tbsp.	green peppercorns, crushed	15 mL
2 cups	sliced Thai basil leaves	475 mL

This is a recipe from the time before chilies were part of Thai cuisine. The peppercorns, cilantro and basil combine with the savory dried shrimp to make an aromatic soup that will take the chill off any winter evening.

Pound or purée the shallots, black peppercorns, cilantro stems and salt. Combine the mixture with the dried shrimp and minced prawns.

Bring the stock to a boil and add the mixture. Stir well and return to a boil.

Add the prawns and vegetables, fish sauce, lime juice and green peppercorns. Boil for a couple of minutes, or until everything is cooked.

Stir in the basil leaves and serve immediately.

Serves 6 to 8.

Salmon, Tamarind and Ginger Soup

Salmon is not typically used in Thai cuisine, but I think it is
the fish best suited to this recipe. The herbs and ginger
complement the salmon perfectly. Any firm-fleshed fish
could be substituted—halibut and monkfish are both great.

Wash the julienned ginger in hot salty water. (This mellows
the hot taste of the ginger.) Drain and set aside.

Using a mortar and pestle, crush the dried shrimp, shallots,
peppercorns, cilantro, 2 tsp. (10 mL) finely chopped ginger
and salt together until a paste is achieved.

Heat the oil in a saucepan over medium heat, add the garlic
and shrimp-shallot paste and fry until fragrant, 1 or 2
minutes. Add the salmon and fry for a couple of minutes.

Add the water or stock, sugar, fish sauce, tamarind water and
julienned ginger. Simmer for about 5 minutes. Taste and
adjust the flavor with more sugar, fish sauce or tamarind
water if necessary. Add the green onion just before serving.

Serves 6.

1 cup	julienned ginger	240 mL
1 Tbsp.	dried shrimp	15 mL
10	shallots	10
15	white peppercorns	15
6 Tbsp.	chopped cilantro stems	90 mL
2 tsp.	finely chopped fresh ginger	10 mL
1/2 tsp.	salt	2.5 mL
1 Tbsp.	oil	15 mL
2	cloves garlic, chopped	2
1 lb.	salmon fillet, diced in 3/4-inch (2-cm) cubes	455 g
6 cups	water or stock	1.5 L
2 Tbsp.	palm or brown sugar	30 mL
4 Tbsp.	fish sauce	60 mL
6 Tbsp.	tamarind water (page 48)	90 mL
1 cup	chopped green onion	240 mL

Vegetarian Tom Yam Soup

6 cups	vegetable stock	1.5 L
2 tsp.	Roasted Chili Paste (page 12)	10 mL
2	stalks lemon grass, sliced into 1-inch (2.5-cm) pieces	2
6	kaffir lime leaves, sliced, or 2 Tbsp. (30 mL) lime zest	6
1/4 cup	soy sauce	60 mL
2 tsp.	sugar	10 mL
1/4 cup	lime juice	60 mL
2	red bell peppers, sliced	2
1 1/3 cups	mushrooms, sliced	320 mL
4–6	small fresh red or greens chilies, slightly crushed	4–6
	cilantro leaves, for garnish	

This version of *Tom Yam* gets a lot of its flavor from the roasted chili paste and mushrooms. Shiitake mushrooms are a good addition to this soup.

In a large pot, bring the vegetable stock to a boil and stir in the chili paste. Add the remaining ingredients, except for the cilantro leaves, and simmer, stirring often, until the mushrooms are just cooked but still al dente.

Pour into a serving bowl and garnish with cilantro leaves.

Serves 4.

Country-Style Hot and Sour Soup

I first saw this soup—*Gaeng Som*—made at the Suan Dusit college culinary program in Bangkok, when I was exchanging recipes with the instructors. The tart flavor comes from the tamarind. This soup is sometimes served as a thin curry with jasmine rice.

Bring the chicken stock to a boil in a soup pot. Add the lemon grass, galanga, lime leaves, curry paste, tamarind water and fish sauce. Simmer for 10 minutes and strain.

Add the vegetables one at a time, in order of hardness and how long they take to cook. Simmer until they're cooked but still crunchy. Add the prawns or chicken and cook until they're done, about 5 minutes.

Stir in the lime juice and serve garnished with cilantro.

Serves 4.

4 cups	chicken stock	950 mL
1	stalk lemon grass, sliced	1
1	1-inch (2.5-cm) piece galanga, sliced	1
4	kaffir lime leaves, sliced	4
1 Tbsp.	Red Curry Paste (page 8)	5 mL / 1
5 Tbsp.	tamarind water (page 48)	75 mL
3 Tbsp.	fish sauce	45 mL
1/2 cup	cauliflower florets	120 mL
1/2 cup	broccoli florets	120 mL
1/3 cup	bok choy, chopped	80 mL
1/3 cup	sui choy, chopped	80 mL
1/4 cup	mushrooms, sliced	60 mL
1/4 cup	snow peas	60 mL
1/4 cup	baby corn	60 mL
8 oz.	prawns or sliced boneless skinless chicken breast	227 g
1 Tbsp.	lime juice	15 mL
1/4 cup	cilantro leaves	60 mL

Salads

Chicken, Prawn and Fruit Salad

2 Tbsp.	oil	30 mL
3	shallots, sliced	3
1/4 lb.	skinless boneless chicken breast, finely diced	113 g
10	raw prawns, peeled	10
1 tsp.	white sugar	5 mL
1 tsp.	fish sauce	5 mL
3 Tbsp.	lime juice	45 mL
1	large green apple, cored and thinly sliced	1
1 cup	seedless green grapes	240 mL
1 cup	seedless red grapes	240 mL
4	cloves garlic, minced	4
3	small red chilies, sliced	3
1	large orange, peeled and sliced	1
1/4 cup	chopped roasted peanuts	60 mL
1/4 cup	sliced cilantro leaves	60 mL

The combination of raw garlic and fried shallots with fresh fruit, chicken and shrimp creates a unique flavor explosion.

Heat the oil over medium-high in a small frying pan. Add the shallots and stir-fry until crispy and golden. Place on paper towels to drain and set aside.

Place the chicken in a small saucepan, cover with water and simmer for about 5 minutes, or until the chicken is cooked. Remove the chicken from the water with a slotted spoon. Add the prawns to the same water. Cook for about 2 to 3 minutes over medium heat. Drain the prawns and slice them into 1/4-inch (.6-cm) pieces. Put the chicken and prawns in a bowl.

In a small bowl, mix the sugar, fish sauce and lime juice together for a dressing.

Reserve some crisp shallots and some cilantro leaves for garnish. Toss the remaining ingredients together with the chicken, prawns and lime juice dressing. Garnish and serve.

Serves 4.

Chopped Chicken Salad

This salad is common throughout most parts of the country and is served in many different ways. It is called *Laarb Gai* (*gai* means "chicken"). I have had this dish made with pork or beef, and once, at a roadside stand in Petchaboon, I had a spectacular plate of *laarb* made with chopped duck. When I make this at home, I often use ground turkey because it is a low-fat alternative. The texture can be varied depending on whether you use ground meat or chop it by hand. Laarb is usually served on a bed of lettuce or chopped cabbage; sometimes it is served with iceberg lettuce leaves so that it can be rolled up into a wrap. My favorite way to eat it is stuffed into hollowed-out chunks of cucumber. The ground toasted rice powder thickens and flavors the mixture. It can be purchased in many Asian markets or you can make your own.

1	long English cucumber	1
1 tsp.	vegetable oil	5 mL
4 Tbsp.	lime juice	60 mL
2 cups	chopped or ground chicken meat	475 mL
3 Tbsp.	toasted rice powder	45 mL
2 Tbsp.	diced shallot	30 mL
1/4 cup	chopped mint leaves	60 mL
2 Tbsp.	chopped cilantro leaves	30 mL
1/2 tsp.	ground chili flakes	2.5 mL
2 Tbsp.	fish sauce	30 mL

Cut the cucumber at a 45-degree angle into 2-inch (5-cm) pieces. Scoop out the center of each piece with a small melon baller or teaspoon. Set aside.

Heat the oil in a wok over medium heat. Mix 2 Tbsp. (30 mL) of the lime juice with the chicken and cook until the chicken is no longer pink.

Turn the heat off and mix in the rice powder, shallot, mint, cilantro, chili, remaining lime juice and fish sauce. Using a teaspoon, fill the hollowed-out cucumber pieces with the chicken mixture.

Serves 4.

How to Make Toasted Rice Powder

Place 1/2 cup (120 mL) of uncooked jasmine rice in a dry, heavy frying pan and cook over medium heat while stirring constantly, until the rice becomes brown and fragrant.

Grind the toasted rice into tiny pieces in a food processor. It will keep for a month in a tightly sealed container.

Southern Thai Bean Thread Noodle and Chicken Salad

8 oz.	dried bean thread noodles	227 g
2 Tbsp.	sesame oil	30 mL
1/2 cup	dried wood ear mushrooms	120 g
2	limes, juiced	2
1 Tbsp.	fish sauce	15 mL
1 Tbsp.	soy sauce	15 mL
1 tsp.	hot sauce	5 mL
1	clove garlic, crushed	1
2 Tbsp.	minced fresh ginger	30 mL
1 Tbsp.	vegetable oil	15 mL
1/2 lb.	assorted fresh mushrooms, sliced	227 g
1/2 lb.	skinless boneless chicken, diced	227 g
3	green onions, sliced	3
1 cup	snow peas	240 mL
1/4 cup	cilantro leaves, chopped	60 mL
1/2 cup	toasted cashews	120 mL

Bean thread noodles are also called glass noodles because they turn transparent when cooked. Wood ear mushrooms can be purchased dry in many Asian markets. They are reconstituted in hot water and have an almost crisp texture. You could substitute dried shiitake mushrooms; they do not have the same texture but they taste great in this salad and are much easier to find. If you like, substitute prawns for the chicken.

Heat 6 cups (1.5 L) water to a boil, drop in the noodles and cook until soft, about 5 minutes. Drain, rinse in cold water and drain again. Toss the noodles in the sesame oil and place in a serving bowl.

Soak the dried mushrooms in hot water for 15 minutes. Drain, slice into thin strips and set aside.

Mix together the lime juice, fish sauce, soy sauce, hot sauce, garlic and 1 Tbsp. (15 mL) of the ginger. Set aside for a dressing.

Heat the vegetable oil in a frying pan over high heat and fry the fresh mushrooms and wood ear mushrooms until the fresh mushrooms start to soften. Add the diced chicken and remaining 1 Tbsp. (15 mL) ginger and fry on high heat for 2 minutes, or until the chicken is no longer pink.

Add the chicken and mushroom mixture to the noodles along with the green onions, snow peas and cilantro.

Toss together with the dressing and chill for 20 minutes. Scatter the cashews on top just before serving.

Serves 4.

Northern Thai Shrimp Salad

This salad is similar to a colorful coleslaw and it is often served in a hollowed-out red cabbage. It is an ideal choice for people wanting a very low-fat dressing, as it is completely oil free. Cooked diced chicken could be substituted for the shrimp.

Combine the lime juice, fish sauce, cayenne powder, minced onion, ginger and water or stock in a pan. Bring to a boil, then lower the heat to a simmer and cook for about 5 minutes. Stir in the green onion, mint and cilantro. Remove from the heat and let cool. The dressing can be refrigerated for up to 2 days.

Toss the remaining ingredients, except for the sliced lettuce, in the dressing just before serving. Place on a bed of sliced lettuce.

Serves 4.

5 Tbsp.	lime juice	75 mL
1/4 cup	fish sauce	60 mL
1/2 tsp.	cayenne powder	2.5 mL
1/2 cup	minced onion	120 mL
1 Tbsp.	chopped fresh ginger	15 mL
1/2 cup	water or stock	120 mL
1/4 cup	chopped green onion	60 mL
2 Tbsp.	sliced mint	30 mL
1/4 cup	sliced cilantro	60 mL
1 lb.	baby shrimp, cooked	455 g
1/2 cup	red cabbage, finely sliced	120 mL
1/2 cup	green cabbage, finely sliced	120 mL
1 cup	grated carrot	240 mL
1 cup	cucumber, finely sliced	240 mL
1 cup	green bell pepper, finely sliced	240 mL
4	large lettuce leaves, sliced	4

Lemon Grass Beef Salad

1/4 oz.	bean thread or thin rice noodles	7 g
1 lb.	steak, such as ribeye or tenderloin	455 g
1	red onion, thinly sliced	1
1	cucumber, thinly sliced	1
1	stalk lemon grass with top and root removed, finely minced	1
1/4 cup	lime juice	60 mL
1 Tbsp.	fish sauce	15 mL
2	small chilies, chopped	2
2	green onions, chopped	2
10	basil leaves, sliced	10
10	mint leaves, sliced	10

This salad is best with the steak cooked on a barbecue because the smoky flavor of the meat adds a great deal to the dish. It is essential to mince the lemon grass until it is very fine. Lemon grass that is not cooked can have the texture of a tree branch if it is in large pieces. If you are unsure of your knife skills, chop the lemon grass as fine as you can, then mince it in a food processor.

Soak the bean thread noodles in hot water for 10 to 15 minutes, or place them in boiling water until tender, drain and plunge immediately into cold water. If you are using rice noodles, see page 132. Drain and cut into 3-inch (7.5-cm) pieces.

Heat the barbecue to high and grill the meat to medium-rare, about 2 minutes per side for a 1-inch-thick (2.5-cm) steak. Let sit for 5 minutes. Slice beef into thin, 2-inch-long (5-cm) strips.

Combine all the ingredients in a large bowl. Serve at room temperature.

Serves 4.

Green Bean Salad with Coconut Milk Dressing

This salad really follows the Thai philosophy of food. It contains a wide array of flavors and textures—sweet, tart, spicy, soft, crisp, cooked, raw and more. These diverse elements combine to make an elegant dish that can be served year round.

1 lb.	green beans, cut in 2-inch (5-cm) pieces	455 g
1/2 cup	coconut milk	120 mL
1 tsp.	oil	5 mL
1	small onion, diced	1
1/2 tsp.	crushed chili flakes	2.5 mL
1	head roasted garlic	1
2 Tbsp.	palm or brown sugar	30 mL
2 Tbsp.	lime juice	30 mL
2 Tbsp.	fish sauce	30 mL
1	red onion, thinly sliced	1
2 cups	shredded lettuce	475 mL
1/4 cup	crispy fried shallots	60 mL

Place the beans in a pot of boiling water and cook until tender but still crisp. Remove the beans to a bowl of ice-cold water to chill them. When they're cool, drain and set aside.

Bring the coconut milk to a boil and set aside.

Heat the oil in a skillet and fry the diced onion over medium heat until it is transparent. Add the chili flakes and fry until the mixture is a golden brown.

Place the onion mixture and coconut milk in a blender, add the roasted garlic, sugar, lime juice and fish sauce and blend until smooth.

Toss the beans and sliced red onion with the coconut dressing. Place the shredded lettuce on a platter, cover with the salad and garnish with crispy fried shallots.

Serves 4.

How to Roast Garlic

Peel the garlic cloves and toss them in a little oil. Bake in an oven at 400°F (200°C), loosely wrapped in foil, for about 45 minutes, or until soft and brown.

Som Tam Green Papaya Salad

1 lb.	green papaya	455 g
1	carrot	1
2 oz.	small dried shrimp	57 g
6	cloves garlic, diced	6
5	small green chilies	5
$^1/_2$ cup	unsalted peanuts, roasted and chopped	120 mL
8	cherry tomatoes, cut in half	8
$^1/_3$ cup	lime juice	80 mL
1 Tbsp.	palm or brown sugar	15 mL
1 Tbsp.	fish sauce	15 mL
2 cups	shredded sui choy or napa cabbage	475 mL

This unusual salad is very popular in Thailand. The unripe papaya has a crisp texture and tart flavor. If green papayas are not available, you can substitute a combination of tart green apple and cucumber. My friend Sanit searched in vain for green papayas when he came for a visit, so he made the salad with Granny Smith apples and it tasted fantastic.

Peel the papaya and carrot and cut them into long thin matchsticks.

Take $^1/_3$ of the papaya and all the shrimp, garlic and chili, and pound, using a mortar and pestle, until the mixture is a little soft.

Toss this mixture with the rest of the papaya, the peanuts, tomatoes, carrot, lime juice, sugar and fish sauce.

Stir the salad vigorously to combine all the flavors and serve on a bed of shredded sui choy or cabbage.

Serves 4.

Peanut Sesame Noodle Salad

This noodle dish is very simple to make and has all the popular flavors of Thai cuisine. I usually serve it in small portions over a bed of shredded lettuce, but it is just as good served warm as an accompaniment to stir-fried dishes.

To make the dressing, mix the oils with the garlic and peanut butter until smooth. Add the chili, sesame seeds, soy sauce and lime juice, and mix well. Season with salt and pepper.

Place the noodles in a large saucepan of boiling water. Boil egg noodles for 3 minutes; rice noodles for 1 minute. Drain the noodles thoroughly and allow them to cool for a couple of minutes.

Add the dressing, cilantro, green onion, carrot and peanuts and toss well to mix. Serve immediately.

Serves 4.

3 Tbsp.	vegetable oil	45 mL
2 Tbsp.	sesame oil	30 mL
1	clove garlic, crushed	1
1 Tbsp.	peanut butter	15 mL
1	small green chili, seeded and very finely chopped	1
3 Tbsp.	toasted sesame seeds	45 mL
1/4 cup	soy sauce	60 mL
2 Tbsp.	lime juice	30 mL
	salt and black pepper to taste	
1 lb.	egg noodles or rice noodles	455 g
1/4 cup	chopped fresh cilantro	60 mL
1 cup	chopped green onion	240 mL
1 cup	grated carrot	240 mL
1/2 cup	roasted peanuts	120 mL

Keow's Roasted Eggplant Salad

6	long purple eggplant (Chinese or Japanese)	6
3 Tbsp.	chopped shallots	45 mL
1/4 cup	lime juice	60 mL
2 Tbsp.	soy sauce	30 mL
1 Tbsp.	white sugar	15 mL
1 tsp.	chopped chilies	5 mL
4	hard-boiled eggs, sliced	4
1 cup	chopped green onions	240 mL
1 cup	sliced cilantro	240 mL
1/2 cup	crispy fried shallots	120 mL

Keow is a charming woman who cooks in the only restaurant on Siboya Island, a small island paradise in the south of Thailand that can only be accessed by a 90-minute boat trip from Krabi. I was immediately taken by the rich smoky flavor of the roasted eggplant, contrasting with the tartness of the lime dressing. I was lucky enough to convince this shy chef to let me into the kitchen to watch her make it from scratch.

Roast the whole eggplants under the broiler or on a barbecue until they're charred and a little soft, turning them once.

Place the eggplants in a large bowl, cover with plastic wrap and allow to cool. Peel off the charred skin and discard. Slice the eggplant into 2-inch (5-cm) chunks.

To make a dressing, mix the chopped shallots, lime juice, soy sauce, sugar and chilies together.

Arrange the eggplant on a platter. Top with the hard-boiled egg slices, green onion and cilantro. Pour the dressing over top. Scatter fried shallots over the salad before serving.

Serves 6.

Cucumber Chili Salad

This salad is traditionally served with fish cakes, but it is a nice contrast to any grilled or fried food. It can be made well in advance of serving and keeps overnight in the fridge.

Combine all the ingredients except for the salt and peanuts. Taste and adjust the seasoning.

Let the mixture sit at room temperature for at least 15 minutes. Garnish with the peanuts.

Serves 4.

3 cups	thinly sliced long English cucumbers	720 mL
$^1/_2$ cup	coarsely chopped shallots or red onion	120 mL
2–4	red chilies, seeded and finely chopped	2–4
1	red bell pepper, diced	1
$^1/_4$ cup	chopped cilantro	60 mL
$^1/_2$ cup	rice vinegar	120 mL
6 Tbsp.	palm or brown sugar	90 mL
2 Tbsp.	fish sauce	30 mL
$^1/_2$ cup	water	120 mL
$^1/_4$ tsp.	salt (optional)	1.2 mL
$^1/_2$ cup	chopped roasted peanuts (optional)	120 mL

Barbecued Duck and Mushroom Fresh Spring Rolls (page 40)

Salmon in Rice Paper Wraps with Coconut Ginger Sauce (page 72)

Som Tam Green Papaya Salad (page 66) and
Chicken and Red Peppers in Red Coconut Curry Sauce (page 94)

Salmon, Tamarind and Ginger Soup (page 55)

Fish and Seafood

Salmon in Rice Paper Wraps with Coconut Ginger Sauce

8	salmon fillets, about 1 inch (2.5 cm) thick, 4 inches (10 cm) long, 2 inches (5 cm) wide	8
8 tsp.	soy sauce	40 mL
8	round rice paper wrappers, 8 inches (20 cm) in diameter	8
16	basil leaves	16
8 tsp.	chopped fresh ginger	40 mL
2 Tbsp.	oil	30 mL
1 recipe	Coconut Ginger Sauce (page 17)	1 recipe

This is not a traditional dish, but I think a Thai person would like the traditional approach of using different textures in one dish. The rice paper becomes crisp when fried, and the salmon inside is soft and moist. The sauce has a creamy texture and ties all the flavors together. I sometimes use this as an appetizer, serving 1 package per person.

Season each piece of salmon with 1 tsp. (5 mL) of soy sauce. Set aside.

Fill a wide shallow pan with warm water and spread a dish towel on a counter. Dip a wrapper in the water for about 10 seconds to soften it, then place on the towel.

Place 2 basil leaves in the center of the rice paper. Place a piece of salmon on top of the basil. Place 1 tsp. (5 mL) of ginger on top of the salmon. Fold the wrap around the salmon to enclose it securely. Place the salmon packages seam-side down on a plate in a single layer. Cover and refrigerate until cooking time; it can be prepared to this point up to 4 hours ahead.

At cooking time heat the oil in a well-seasoned or non-stick skillet over high heat and place the salmon packages seam-side down in the skillet. Cook uncovered for 2 minutes. Turn over and cook for an additional 2 minutes. Remove the skillet from the heat, cover and set aside for 3 or 4 minutes while you make the sauce.

Place $1/4$ of the sauce on each plate. Place the wraps seam-side down so the basil leaves show through the rice paper.

Serves 4.

Salmon Baked in Banana Leaves

The salmon steams inside the banana leaf and the fish juices combine with the flavoring ingredients to create a unique sauce. Any firm-fleshed fish can be substituted for salmon. You can make the packages up to an hour ahead of cooking.

Preheat the oven to 375°F (190°C).

Mix the curry paste, coconut cream, sugar, fish sauce, basil and lime leaves together. Coat each salmon fillet with the mixture. Place each coated fillet on a banana leaf. Fold the leaf to completely enclose the salmon. Pin together with toothpicks.

Place the packages on a cookie sheet, set in the oven and bake for about 15 minutes.

Serves 4.

4 tsp.	Red Curry Paste (page 8)	20 mL
1/2 cup	coconut cream (the thick top portion of canned coconut milk)	120 mL
2 Tbsp.	palm or brown sugar	30 mL
1 Tbsp.	fish sauce	15 mL
1/2 cup	sliced basil leaves	120 mL
8	kaffir lime leaves, finely sliced, or 1 Tbsp. (15 mL) lime zest	8
4	salmon fillets, about 6 oz. (170 g) each	4
4	frozen banana leaves, about 12 x 14 inches (30 x 35 cm), defrosted (see page 153)	4

Roasted Rock Fish with Coconut and Mango

For the spice paste:

1/2 cup	chopped onion	120 mL
2	cloves garlic	2
4	dried chilies	4
2 Tbsp.	chopped cilantro stems	30 mL
1 Tbsp.	chopped galanga	15 mL
1 Tbsp.	tamarind water (page 48)	15 mL
1/2 tsp.	black pepper	2.5 mL

For the coconut sauce:

2 tsp.	hot sauce	10 mL
2 Tbsp.	fish sauce	30 mL
2 Tbsp.	rice vinegar	30 mL
2 Tbsp.	palm or brown sugar	30 mL
1 cup	coconut milk	240 mL

For the roasted rock fish:

1	2-lb. (900-g) whole rock cod or snapper	1
2 cups	shredded sui choy or napa cabbage	475 mL
2	stalks lemon grass	2
4	star anise	4
4	kaffir lime leaves	4

For the garnish:

1	mango, sliced	1
1/4 cup	sliced cilantro	60 mL

This dish is rich with complex layers of flavor. The sweet mango complements the spiciness of the fish nicely. Salmon is an ideal substitute for rock fish, but most types of whole fish can be cooked with this method.

Pulse the spice paste ingredients to a paste in a food processor, or pound them in a mortar and pestle.

Place the coconut sauce ingredients in a saucepan and bring to a boil. Set aside.

Preheat the oven to 425°F (220°C).

Make 4 slashes on each side of the fish. Spread the spice paste into the cavity of the fish as well as all over the surface. Place in a non-reactive dish and marinate in the fridge for 2 hours.

Place a doubled sheet of aluminum foil on a counter and put the cabbage in a band down the middle. Place the fish on top. Lightly bruise the lemon grass, star anise and lime leaves and place in the cavity of the fish.

Turn up the edges of the foil. Pour the coconut sauce over the fish. Seal the foil, and place the parcel on a baking sheet. Place in the oven and bake for 30 minutes.

Transfer the fish to a platter. Scatter the mango and cilantro on top.

Serves 4.

Monkfish in Green Coconut Curry Sauce

Use any firm-fleshed fish such as halibut, salmon or sea bass in this dish. I often make it with a mixture of different types of fish and add prawns and scallops.

Heat 2 tsp. (10 mL) of the oil in a wok over high heat. Add the green pepper and onion and sauté for about 5 minutes. Remove and set aside.

Heat the remaining 1 tsp. (5 mL) of oil in the wok. Add the curry paste and sauté on high heat for 2 minutes. Add the coconut milk and bring to a boil. Lower the temperature to medium and cook for 5 minutes.

Add the sugar and fish sauce. Add the sautéed onions and peppers and the kaffir lime leaves. Cook for 5 minutes, then add the monkfish and simmer for another 5 minutes.

Add the basil leaves just before serving. Serve with rice.

Serves 4.

3 tsp.	oil	15 mL
2	green bell peppers, sliced	2
1	large onion, sliced	1
¼ cup	Green Curry Paste (page 9)	60 mL
4 cups	coconut milk	950 mL
2 tsp.	palm or brown sugar	10 mL
3 Tbsp.	fish sauce	45 mL
6	kaffir lime leaves, sliced	6
1½ lbs.	monkfish fillet, cubed	680 g
½ cup	sliced Thai basil leaves	120 mL

Grilled Pomfret with Tamarind Chili Sauce

2 lbs.	whole pomfret, cleaned, head and tail on	900 g
2 Tbsp.	soy sauce	30 mL

Fish with this type of chili sauce can be found all over central and southern Thailand. Pomfret is a very popular fish in Southeast Asia and it is now available frozen in many Western cities. Most types of whole fish could be substituted and I often make this recipe with fresh talapia. The tamarind chili sauce can be made a day before serving.

Cut 3 slashes into the meat of the fish on both sides. Rub the soy sauce over the fish. Grill for 4 minutes on each side over a hot barbecue or under a broiler in the oven.

Serve on a platter covered with the tamarind chili sauce.

Serves 4.

Tamarind Chili Sauce

2 Tbsp.	vegetable oil	30 mL
6	cloves garlic, diced	6
10	shallots, peeled and diced	10
2 tsp.	chopped cilantro stems	10 mL
5	red chilies, diced	5
1 Tbsp.	palm or brown sugar	15 mL
3 Tbsp.	tamarind water (page 48)	45 mL
1 Tbsp.	fish sauce	15 mL

Heat the oil in a wok over high heat. Stir-fry the garlic, shallots, cilantro and chilies until the garlic starts to brown. Turn off the heat and stir in the sugar, tamarind, water and fish sauce.

Makes about $1/3$ cup (80 mL).

Grilled Squid with Tamarind Chili Sauce

Street vendors grilling squid over hot coals is a common sight in a Thai city or town. This is one of many versions. It could be done under a broiler in the oven, but I would miss the charred smoky flavor.

Make a marinade by pounding the garlic, white peppercorns, cilantro, ginger, soy sauce and oil together in a mortar and pestle.

Slice down the side of each squid tube and open it up so it lies flat. Score the squid with a sharp knife in a criss-cross pattern. This will help to keep it from curling on the grill.

Rub the squid with the marinade. Set it aside to marinate for 15 minutes.

Grill the squid for 1 minute on each side over a hot barbecue. Serve with Tamarind Chili Sauce.

Serves 4.

2	cloves garlic, chopped	2
1/2 tsp.	crushed white peppercorns	2.5 mL
1 Tbsp.	chopped cilantro stems	15 mL
1/2 tsp.	chopped fresh ginger	2.5 mL
2 Tbsp.	soy sauce	30 mL
1 Tbsp.	vegetable oil	15 mL
1 1/2 lbs.	squid tubes	680 g
1 recipe	Tamarind Chili Sauce (page 76)	1 recipe

Baa Wan's Squid Stir-fry

1	egg	1
1 Tbsp.	chili oil	15 mL
2 tsp.	curry powder	10 mL
1 Tbsp.	coconut milk	15 mL
1 Tbsp.	Maggi seasoning sauce	15 mL
1 tsp.	white sugar	5 mL
1 Tbsp.	vegetable oil	15 mL
1	onion, cut in thin wedges	1
1	red bell pepper, sliced into strips	1
1	stalk celery, thinly sliced	1
2	green onions, sliced	2
	a few celery leaves	
1 lb.	squid, sliced into strips	455 g

The last time I was in Thailand I spent some time in the kitchen of a restaurant in Bangkok with some cooks who were willing to show me their version of traditional Thai dishes. The head chef was a cheerful lady nicknamed Baa Wan. I later learned that this means "fat aunt." Although I didn't think she was fat, she was a little rounder than the other typically slight Asian ladies in the kitchen. Do not overcook the squid in this dish. The longer it is cooked, the more rubbery the texture becomes. When cooked properly, it should be very soft.

Stir the egg, chili oil, curry powder, coconut milk, Maggi seasoning sauce and sugar together in a small bowl. Set aside.

Heat the vegetable oil in a wok over medium heat and fry the onion, red pepper, celery, green onion and celery leaves for 2 minutes. Add the squid and fry for 1 more minute.

Add the sauce mixture, raise the heat to high, and cook for another 1 to 2 minutes.

Serves 4.

Red Snapper and Prawns in Lemon Grass Coconut Curry Sauce

You can make this dish with most types of fish. The spice paste and marinade can be made several days ahead and refrigerated.

Process all the spice paste ingredients in a food processor till smooth. Set aside.

Mix all the marinade ingredients together.

Cover the snapper and prawns with the marinade and place in the fridge for 15 minutes.

Heat the oil in a wok over high heat. Fry the spice paste for 30 seconds. Add $^1/_2$ cup (120 mL) of the coconut milk and the lemon grass and bring to a boil. Lower the heat and simmer for 5 minutes.

Remove the lemon grass. Add the marinated fish and prawns, the lime juice and tamarind water. Cook the fish and prawns for about 1 minute. Add the rest of the coconut milk and simmer for 5 minutes. Add water if desired to thin the sauce.

Serves 6.

For the spice paste:

4	dried chilies, chopped	4
1	small onion, chopped	1
2	cloves garlic	2
4	stalks lemon grass, thinly sliced	4
1 tsp.	shrimp paste	5 mL

For the marinade:

$^1/_2$ cup	coconut milk	120 mL
1 Tbsp.	curry powder	15 mL
2 Tbsp.	white sugar	30 mL
1 tsp.	salt	5 mL
1 tsp.	fish sauce	5 mL

For the snapper and prawns in curry sauce:

2 lbs.	red snapper fillets, cubed	900 g
1 lb.	tiger prawns, shelled	455 g
1 Tbsp.	oil	15 mL
$1^1/_2$ cups	coconut milk	360 mL
2	stalks lemon grass, lightly pounded	2
$^1/_4$ cup	lime juice	60 mL
$^1/_2$ cup	tamarind water (page 48)	120 mL

Chili Garlic Prawns with Asparagus

2 Tbsp.	vegetable oil	30 mL
1	onion, sliced into small wedges	1
1/2 lb.	asparagus tips, about 3 inches (7.5 cm) long	227 g
5	cloves garlic, diced	5
4	dried whole red chilies	4
14 oz.	tiger prawns, shells removed	400 g
1/2	red bell pepper, diced	1/2
1 Tbsp.	fish sauce	15 mL
1/4 cup	chicken stock	60 mL
1/2 tsp.	crushed black pepper	2.5 mL

This simple stir-fry relies on the natural flavors of the ingredients. Like most stir-fry dishes, this one shows the influence of Chinese cuisine. The fresh taste and aromas are a result of quick cooking over high heat. The asparagus tips should still be a little crunchy and bright green. The dried chilies are left whole so they add a subtle heat to the dish that does not overwhelm the prawns.

Heat 1 Tbsp. (15 mL) of the oil in a wok over high heat, add the onion and asparagus and stir-fry until they start to soften, about 2 minutes.

Push the onion and asparagus up the sides of the wok. Add the remaining oil to the center of the wok. Add the garlic and chilies and stir-fry for 30 seconds.

Add the prawns and stir-fry for 1 minute. Stir in the bell pepper, fish sauce, chicken stock and black pepper. Cook for 1 more minute. Serve with rice.

Serves 4.

Tiger Prawns with Thai Herb Pesto Sauce

This is a fusion of the cuisines of Italy and Thailand. The herb blend explodes with fresh flavors. When cooked into the velvety coconut sauce it is a most elegant comfort food.

1 cup	thick coconut milk	240 mL
1 lb.	tiger prawns, shelled	455 g
1 tsp.	fish sauce	5 mL
1/2 cup	Thai Herb Pesto Sauce	120 mL

Heat the coconut milk to the boiling point. Add the prawns and lower the heat to medium. Cook the prawns for 1 to 2 minutes, depending on the size.

Turn the heat off before swirling the fish sauce and the pesto sauce into the coconut milk. Serve the prawns and sauce over toast points or tossed with hot pasta.

Serves 4.

Thai Herb Pesto Sauce

Heat the oil in a pan and cook the almonds on high heat for about 2 minutes until toasted. Remove the nuts with a slotted spoon and drain on a paper towel. Reserve the oil.

In a food processor, grind the nuts and add the chili, ginger and garlic. Mix briefly and add the basil, spinach, cilantro, mint, lime juice, fish or soy sauce and the reserved oil. Add stock to moisten the mixture if necessary. Mix briefly. The pesto blend can be made ahead and frozen for up to one month.

Makes about 2 cups (475 mL).

2 Tbsp.	vegetable oil	30 mL
2 Tbsp.	almonds	30 mL
1	small green chili, diced	1
1	3/4-inch (2-cm) piece fresh ginger, finely chopped	1
2	cloves garlic, finely diced	2
1 cup	basil leaves	240 mL
1/2 cup	spinach leaves	120 mL
3/4 cup	cilantro leaves	180 mL
1/4 cup	mint leaves	60 mL
2 Tbsp.	lime juice	30 mL
1 tsp.	fish sauce or soy sauce	5 mL
1/3 cup	stock (fish, chicken or vegetable)	80 mL

Prawns with Ginger Cream Sauce

$^1/_4$ cup	olive oil	60 mL
2 Tbsp.	Red Curry Paste (page 8)	30 mL
2 lbs.	tiger prawns, shelled	900 g
1 Tbsp.	olive oil	15 mL
$1^1/_2$ tsp.	mild chili powder	7.5 mL
1 recipe	Ginger Cream Sauce (page 23)	1 recipe
2 tsp.	chili powder	10 mL

This is my version of a dish that I first had in California. It is an interesting combination of French and Thai ingredients and technique.

Combine the $^1/_4$ cup (60 mL) olive oil and the curry paste in a large mixing bowl and whisk to blend well. Add the prawns and toss gently until completely coated. Cover the bowl with plastic wrap and marinate in the fridge for 2 hours.

Heat the 1 Tbsp. (15 mL) olive oil in a large skillet over high heat. Add the prawns and sear for 2 to 3 minutes on each side. Sprinkle with the chili powder.

Combine $^1/_3$ cup (80 mL) of the ginger cream sauce and the 2 tsp. (10 mL) chili powder in a small squeeze bottle. Shake well to blend.

Divide the remaining ginger cream sauce among 4 serving plates, smoothing the sauce over the entire bottom of the plate. Arrange $^1/_4$ of the prawns in the center of each plate. Squeeze lines of the chili cream sauce mixture around the prawns in a bull's-eye pattern. Gently stroke across the lines with the point of a knife to create spokes radiating out from the prawns. Serve immediately.

Serves 4.

Phuket Prawns

Phuket is a coastal resort area in southern Thailand known for its white sand beaches and fresh seafood. Flying over Phuket, I saw dozens of what looked like small lakes dotting the coastline. These turned out to be prawn farms, which supply most North American restaurants with the famous Thai black tiger prawns. This dish is typical of the kind of meal you would see quickly stir-fried by a street vendor in a Phuket outdoor market. It makes a simple yet exotic lunch with steamed rice.

6 Tbsp.	vegetable oil	90 mL
1 lb.	tiger prawns, shelled	455 g
4	cloves garlic, finely diced	4
$^1/_2$ cup	thinly sliced green bell pepper	120 mL
$^1/_2$ cup	thinly sliced red bell pepper	120 mL
$^1/_2$ cup	thinly sliced mushrooms	120 mL
$^1/_2$ cup	thinly sliced onion	120 mL
$^1/_2$ cup	Thai basil leaves	120 mL
2 tsp.	curry powder	10 mL
$^1/_4$ cup	fish sauce	60 mL
2 Tbsp.	oyster sauce	30 mL
3 Tbsp.	sugar	45 mL

Heat 4 Tbsp. (60 mL) of the oil in a wok over high heat until it's almost smoking. Add the prawns and garlic and stir-fry for 1 minute. Remove the prawns and keep warm.

Heat the remaining 2 Tbsp. (30 mL) of oil in the same wok. Add the remaining ingredients and stir-fry on high heat for about 2 minutes. The mushrooms should release their liquid and soften.

Return the prawns to the wok and stir-fry for 1 more minute. Serve immediately with steamed rice.

Serves 4.

Lemon Grass Curried Mussels

2 Tbsp.	vegetable oil	30 mL
2	onions, diced	2
2	cloves garlic, diced	2
2 Tbsp.	chopped fresh ginger	30 mL
1 Tbsp.	curry powder	15 mL
3	stalks lemon grass, trimmed and sliced into 2-inch (5-cm) pieces	3
1 cup	chopped cilantro	240 mL
1/2 tsp.	fresh cracked black pepper	2.5 mL
1 Tbsp.	palm or brown sugar	15 mL
1/4 cup	lime juice	60 mL
1 cup	dry white wine	240 mL
4 lbs.	mussels in the shell	1.8 kg

This citrus-infused dish is typical of the kind of food served in restaurants on the white sand beaches of southern Thailand.

In a large pot or a wok, heat the oil over high heat. Add the onion, garlic, ginger and curry powder and sauté until the onions are soft. Add the lemon grass, cilantro, pepper, sugar, lime juice and wine and bring to a boil.

Add the mussels and cover the pot. Boil until the shells open, about 5 minutes. Discard any that do not open.

Serve the cooking liquid as a sauce with the mussels.

Serves 4.

Seared Scallops and Basil Mango Sauce

The mango sauce has a luxurious texture and sweet fruit flavor that goes well with the seared scallops. The color contrasts are spectacular when served with black rice.

2	very ripe mangos, peeled, seeded and chopped	2
2 cups	orange juice	475 mL
1/2 cup	chopped Thai basil	120 mL
2 Tbsp.	oil	30 mL
2 lbs.	scallops (medium or large)	900 g

Place the mango in a food processor and purée (or use canned). You should have almost 2 cups (475 mL) of purée. Add the orange juice and pulse until combined. Stir in the chopped basil. Set aside.

Heat the oil in a large heavy skillet until it is almost smoking. Add the scallops in one layer. Cook for about 1 minute, until slightly brown on the bottom. Turn over and cook the other side for another minute. Cooking times will vary according to the size of the scallops. Be careful not to cook them too long! When they are browned on both sides, they are ready.

Remove the scallops from the pan and keep warm. Add the mango sauce to the pan and heat for 1 minute. To serve, place a spoonful of sauce under each scallop.

Serve immediately.

Serves 4.

Whiskey and Coconut Marinated
Seared Scallops

1	clove garlic, minced	1
1/8 tsp.	crushed white pepper	.5 mL
6 Tbsp.	whiskey	90 mL
3 Tbsp.	coconut cream	45 mL
1 Tbsp.	Red Curry Paste (page 8)	15 mL
1 lb.	large scallops	455 g
2 tsp.	vegetable oil	10 mL
1/2 cup	coconut milk	120 mL
1 tsp.	palm or brown sugar	5 mL
2 tsp.	fish sauce	10 mL
1/2 cup	sliced green onions	120 mL
3 Tbsp.	chopped fresh basil	45 mL

Searing the scallops in a very hot pan and cooking them quickly in the sauce is essential in this recipe. If the pan is not hot enough, the scallops will not caramelize on the bottom and they will shrink and get tough. The whiskey and basil create an incredible aroma that is infused into the scallops.

Combine the garlic, pepper, 3 Tbsp. (45 mL) of the whiskey, coconut cream and curry paste. Add the scallops and marinate for 15 minutes.

Heat the oil in a heavy skillet until it's almost smoking. Add the scallops and stir-fry for 1 to 2 minutes. Lower the heat to medium and add the coconut milk, sugar, fish sauce, remaining 3 Tbsp. (45 mL) whiskey, green onions and basil. Cook for 1 more minute.

Serves 4.

Steamed Seafood Custard

This dish—called *Hor Muk*—is usually served in small, one-cup portions made out of a folded banana leaf. The filled banana-leaf cups are then placed in a bamboo steamer. The larger casserole version is more practical for Western kitchens. *Hor Muk* is often made without the chilies as a food for young children.

Preheat the oven to 400°F (200°C).

Purée the fish fillets in a food processor. Mix $^3/_4$ cup (180 mL) of the coconut milk with the curry paste. Add the fish purée and combine thoroughly. Stir in the eggs, seafood, fish sauce and salt. Mix well.

Line a casserole dish with the banana leaves and scatter the basil leaves over the top of the banana leaves. Spoon the fish mixture over the basil leaves.

Place the casserole dish in a baking pan filled with hot water, place in the oven and bake for 20 minutes.

Combine the remaining coconut milk with the rice flour and spread over the top of the seafood casserole. Sprinkle the lime leaves and red chili over the coconut rice flour topping and bake for another 5 minutes.

Serves 4.

$^3/_4$ lb.	fish fillets, such as sole or snapper	340 g
1$^1/_2$ cups	coconut milk	360 mL
2 Tbsp.	Red Curry Paste (page 8)	30 mL
2	eggs, lightly beaten	2
$^1/_4$ lb.	assorted seafood, such as prawns or scallops	113 g
1 Tbsp.	fish sauce	15 mL
1 tsp.	salt	5 mL
4	frozen banana leaves, about 12 x 14 inches (30 x 35 cm), defrosted (see page 153)	4
1 cup	Thai basil leaves	240 mL
1 Tbsp.	rice flour	15 mL
2	kaffir lime leaves, finely shredded	2
2	red chilies, thinly sliced	2

Poultry

Lime and Honey Roasted Duck

¹/₄ cup	honey	60 mL
1 Tbsp.	lime juice	15 mL
1 Tbsp.	soy sauce	15 mL
1 tsp.	finely chopped fresh ginger	5 mL
2 tsp.	5-spice powder	10 mL
4	boneless duck breasts	4
	salt and black pepper to taste	
1 Tbsp.	vegetable oil	15 mL

This dish is another example of the influence from China. Five-spice powder is a blend of spices used to flavor meats. It is available in most Asian markets but I have included a recipe to make your own. When it is freshly ground, it has infinitely more flavor than the store-bought version. Traditionally, duck would be roasted whole, but this method is quick and easy. The dish is a perfect match for Lemon Grass Risotto (page 124).

Preheat the oven to 375°F (190°C). Mix the honey, lime juice, soy sauce, ginger and 5-spice powder together in a small bowl and set aside.

Season the duck breasts with salt and pepper. Heat the oil in a heavy skillet over high heat. Brown the duck breasts on both sides.

Remove the duck to a baking sheet and coat with the honey mixture. Bake for 15 to 20 minutes, basting occasionally with the juices.

Serves 4.

5-Spice Powder

1 Tbsp.	star anise	15 mL
1 Tbsp.	Szechuan peppercorns	15 mL
1 tsp.	cinnamon	5 mL
1 Tbsp.	fennel seeds	15 mL
1 tsp.	cloves	5 mL

Pound all the spices together in a mortar and pestle or grind in a spice grinder. This makes about ¹/₄ cup (60 mL) and will keep in a tightly sealed jar for up to 2 months.

Pineapple Chicken and Cashews in Banana Leaves

Cooking food in banana leaves is similar to the French style of cooking *en papillotte*—in parchment paper. The main difference is that the banana leaves infuse the food with an earthy herb flavor that is nothing like the taste of banana. This dish would still taste good if you had to use parchment or foil instead of banana leaves.

Preheat the oven to 400°F (200°C).

In a large bowl whisk together the curry paste, coconut milk, stock, sugar and fish sauce. Toss the chicken, cashews, pineapple, basil and green onions in the curry paste mixture.

Place the chicken mixture on a banana leaf. Cover with the second banana leaf. Fold to completely enclose the chicken mixture and pin together with toothpicks.

Place on a baking sheet and bake for 20 minutes.

Serves 4.

2 Tbsp.	Red Curry Paste (page 8)	30 mL
¹/₂ cup	coconut milk	120 mL
¹/₂ cup	chicken stock	120 mL
2 Tbsp.	palm or brown sugar	30 mL
1 Tbsp.	fish sauce	15 mL
1 lb.	skinless boneless chicken breasts, cut in 1-inch (2.5-cm) cubes	227 g
¹/₂ cup	toasted cashews	120 mL
1 cup	pineapple tidbits	240 mL
¹/₄ cup	chopped fresh basil	60 mL
1 cup	sliced green onions	240 mL
2	frozen banana leaves, about 12 x 14 inches (30 x 35 cm), defrosted (see page 153)	2

Massaman Chicken Curry

4 cups	coconut milk	950 mL
2 lbs.	chicken thighs, bone in	900 g
2	onions, cut in wedges	2
1	red bell pepper, sliced	1
1 cup	roasted peanuts	240 mL
2 tsp.	salt	10 mL
3 Tbsp.	Massaman Curry Paste (page 11)	45 mL
3 Tbsp.	fish sauce	45 mL
1 Tbsp.	tamarind water (page 48)	15 mL
1 Tbsp.	palm or brown sugar	15 mL

This is a southern-style curry that is now popular all over Thailand. The fragrant Middle Eastern spices show the influence from Malaysia and give this dish its distinctive taste and aroma. Beef is sometimes used instead of chicken.

Bring the coconut milk to a boil in a large saucepan. Add the chicken, onion, red pepper, peanuts and salt. Simmer for 40 minutes, or until the chicken is tender.

Remove $1/2$ cup (120 mL) of the coconut milk and bring it to a boil in a frying pan. Add the curry paste and cook for 1 minute.

Return the curry coconut milk to the pot with the chicken. Add the fish sauce, tamarind water and sugar and simmer for another 10 to 15 minutes.

Serves 6.

Lime and Tamarind Chicken

The flavors of the lime, lemon grass and tamarind give a multi-layered citrus taste to this dish that tempers the richness of the coconut milk.

Mix the coconut milk, curry powder, sugar, salt and fish sauce together. Add the chicken, cover, and refrigerate for half an hour.

Grind all the spice paste ingredients together in a food processor until smooth.

Heat the oil in a wok over high heat. Add the spice paste and fry for 30 seconds. Add $^1/_2$ cup (120 mL) of the coconut milk and the lemon grass and bring to a boil.

Add the marinated chicken, lime juice and tamarind water. Stir-fry the chicken until cooked, about 5 minutes. Add the rest of the coconut milk and simmer for 5 minutes. Add water if desired to thin the sauce.

Serves 6.

For the marinade:

$^1/_2$ cup	coconut milk	120 mL
1 Tbsp.	curry powder	15 mL
2 Tbsp.	white sugar	30 mL
1 tsp.	salt	5 mL
1 tsp.	fish sauce	5 mL
3 lbs.	skinless boneless chicken breasts, sliced	1.4 kg

For the spice paste:

4	dried chilies, chopped	4
1	small onion, chopped	1
2	cloves garlic	2
4	stalks lemon grass, thinly sliced	4
1 tsp.	shrimp paste	5 mL

For the lime and tamarind sauce:

1 Tbsp.	oil	15 mL
$1^1/_2$ cups	coconut milk	360 mL
2	stalks lemon grass, lightly pounded	2
$^1/_4$ cup	lime juice	60 mL
$^1/_2$ cup	tamarind water (page 48)	120 mL

Chicken and Red Peppers in Red Coconut Curry Sauce

4 tsp.	oil	20 mL
1	large onion, sliced in wedges	1
1	large red bell pepper, sliced in 2-inch (5-cm) pieces	1
4–6 Tbsp.	Red Curry Paste (page 8)	60–90mL
3 cups	coconut milk	720 mL
2 Tbsp.	fish sauce	30 mL
2 tsp.	palm or brown sugar	10 mL
1 lb.	skinless boneless chicken, cut in 1-inch (2.5-cm) cubes	455 g
5	kaffir lime leaves, sliced	5
1/2 cup	sliced Thai basil leaves	120 mL

Red curry chicken is the most common curry dish in Thailand. This dish has numerous possibilities for variations—beef or seafood instead of chicken and any kind of vegetable instead of red peppers (beans and mushrooms are excellent). Instead of boneless chicken, try a whole cut-up chicken on the bone and simmer the chicken in the sauce for 45 minutes. Then add the fried red pepper and onion. A whole chicken will make a much more flavorful sauce than boneless chicken. The amount of curry paste you use will depend on how hot you have made your curry paste and how spicy you want the dish to be.

Heat 2 tsp. (10 mL) of the oil over medium heat in a wok or frying pan. Add the onion and red pepper and fry until the onion softens. Remove the vegetables and set aside.

Heat the remaining 2 tsp. (10 mL) oil over medium heat in the same wok. Add the red curry paste and fry for about 2 minutes. Add the coconut milk and bring to a boil. Let the sauce boil for 2 to 3 minutes, stirring occasionally, then add the fish sauce and sugar. Return the vegetables to the pan, add the chicken and lime leaves to the sauce and simmer until the chicken is cooked, about 10 minutes.

Chop the basil and add it to the curry just before serving.

Serves 4.

Rama Spinach Chicken Curry

This curry has a rich creamy texture as a result of the spinach cooking into the sauce. A simple vegetable stir-fry makes a nice accompaniment.

Place the coconut milk in a saucepan over medium heat, add the chicken and cook for about 10 minutes, until the chicken is cooked through. Remove the chicken and keep warm.

Add the curry paste, fish sauce, sugar and peanuts to the same coconut milk. Cook over medium heat, stirring constantly, for 10 minutes.

Add the spinach, return the chicken to the coconut milk and stir until warm.

Serve with rice or noodles.

Serves 4.

2	14-oz. (398-mL) cans coconut milk	2
1 lb.	skinless boneless chicken breast, diced	455 g
4 Tbsp.	Red Curry Paste (page 8)	60 mL
2 Tbsp.	fish sauce	30 mL
3 Tbsp.	palm or brown sugar	45 mL
2 cups	chopped roasted peanuts	475 mL
2	10-oz. (284-g) packages frozen chopped spinach, thawed	2

Roasted Chili Paste Chicken and Peanuts in Banana Leaves

2 Tbsp.	Roasted Chili Paste (page 12)	30 mL
1/4 cup	tamarind water (page 48)	60 mL
1/2 cup	water or stock	120 mL
2 Tbsp.	palm or brown sugar	30 mL
1 Tbsp.	fish sauce	15 mL
1 lb.	skinless boneless chicken breasts, cut in 1-inch (2.5-cm) cubes	227 g
1/2 cup	roasted peanuts	120 mL
1 cup	sliced green onions	240 mL
2	frozen banana leaves, about 12 x 14 inches (30 x 35 cm), defrosted (see page 153)	2

This is another dish that derives some of its flavor from banana leaves. Baking in banana leaves is a low-fat cooking method that can be adapted to many other dishes. Most Thai kitchens do not have ovens and these banana leaf packages would typically be cooked on a grill over hot coals.

Preheat the oven to 400°F (200°C).

In a large bowl, stir together the chili paste, tamarind water, water or stock, sugar and fish sauce. Toss the chicken, peanuts and green onions in the mixture.

Place the chicken mixture on a banana leaf. Cover with the second leaf. Fold to completely enclose the chicken and pin it together with toothpicks.

Place on a baking sheet and bake for 15 minutes.

Serves 4.

Spicy Mint Chicken

This is another quick stir-fry showing the Chinese influence on Thai cuisine. One significant difference is that if this dish were cooked in China, the stock would be thickened with cornstarch. Mint is a very popular addition to Thai dishes; Thai basil is sometimes substituted for it or combined with it. The black bean and garlic sauce can be purchased in most Asian markets.

Heat the vegetable oil in a medium skillet over high heat. Add the red onions and garlic and sauté until lightly browned, about $1\frac{1}{2}$ minutes.

Add the chicken and chili pepper and stir-fry for 2 minutes. Add all the remaining ingredients except the mint sprigs and cook, stirring constantly, for 3 minutes. Transfer to a platter and garnish with mint.

Serves 2 to 4.

6 Tbsp.	vegetable oil	90 mL
2 Tbsp.	chopped red onions	30 mL
2 Tbsp.	finely chopped garlic	30 mL
$1\frac{1}{4}$ lbs.	skinless boneless chicken breast, sliced	565 g
$1\frac{1}{2}$ tsp.	finely chopped red chili	7.5 mL
1 cup	thinly sliced onions	240 mL
$\frac{1}{2}$ cup	diced red bell pepper	120 mL
$\frac{1}{2}$ cup	diced tomatoes	120 mL
1 Tbsp.	fish sauce	15 mL
1 Tbsp.	black bean and garlic sauce	15 mL
$1\frac{1}{2}$ tsp.	Maggi seasoning sauce	7.5 mL
$\frac{1}{2}$ cup	chicken stock	120 mL
$\frac{1}{2}$ cup	chopped mint leaves	60 mL
4	sprigs mint, for garnish	4

Northern-Style Marinated Chicken with Sweet Tomato Chutney

12	small chicken thighs, bone in	12
4	cloves garlic, crushed	4
2 Tbsp.	minced fresh ginger	30 mL
2 tsp.	hot sauce	10 mL
3 Tbsp.	dark soy sauce	45 mL
2 Tbsp.	palm or brown sugar	30 mL
2 Tbsp.	rice vinegar	30 mL
2 tsp.	curry powder	10 mL
1 tsp.	ground coriander	5 mL
1/2 tsp.	cinnamon	2.5 mL
1 recipe	Sweet Tomato Chutney	1 recipe

Spicy barbecued chicken is popular throughout the north of Thailand. The tomato chutney is an unusual condiment, as tomatoes are rarely used in Thai cuisine. This dish is traditionally served with a sweet chili sauce. The chutney can be made several days in advance, if kept refrigerated.

Cut slashes in the sides of the chicken thighs. Make a marinade by mixing all the remaining ingredients, except the chutney, together. Toss the chicken in the marinade and place in the fridge for 4 hours or up to overnight.

Preheat the oven to 425ºF (220ºC). Transfer the chicken and marinade to a roasting pan and bake for 40 minutes, or grill the chicken on a barbecue at medium heat for 30 to 40 minutes. Turn and baste the chicken several times as it cooks. Serve with the chutney.

Serves 4.

Sweet Tomato Chutney

2 Tbsp.	oil	30 mL
10	shallots, sliced	10
1	clove garlic, chopped	1
1 tsp.	chopped fresh ginger	5 mL
1/3 cup	rice vinegar	80 mL
2 Tbsp.	sherry or mirin or white wine	30 mL
1/4 cup	palm or brown sugar	60 mL
1 cup	diced tomatoes	240 mL
2 Tbsp.	sweet soy sauce (kecap manis)	30 mL

Heat the oil in a saucepan over high heat. Add the shallots, garlic and ginger and fry until brown. Add the vinegar, sherry, mirin or wine, sugar and 1/4 cup (60 mL) water. Bring to a boil and boil for 10 minutes.

Add the tomatoes and soy sauce and simmer for 5 to 10 minutes.

Makes about 2 cups (475 mL).

Spicy Chicken, Basil and Pepper Stir-fry

Many versions of this dish can be found in Thai homes and restaurants. It is cooked quickly and has a fresh aromatic quality. Basil is the dominant flavor in this dish and I recommend that you make it only with fresh basil.

Heat the oil in a wok over high heat. Add the onion and green peppers and sauté for about 2 minutes. Add the garlic, chicken and chili peppers and sauté for another 2 minutes.

Add all the other ingredients and continue to stir-fry another couple of minutes, or until the chicken is cooked.

Serves 4.

2 tsp.	oil	10 mL
1	onion, sliced in wedges	1
1	green bell pepper, sliced in small wedges	1
2	cloves garlic, diced	2
1 lb.	skinless boneless chicken, diced	455 g
3	small red chilies, diced	3
1 Tbsp.	fish sauce	15 mL
1 Tbsp.	oyster sauce	15 mL
1 Tbsp.	palm or brown sugar	15 mL
1/2 cup	chicken stock	120 mL
1 cup	sliced Thai basil leaves	240 mL

Thai Whiskey Peppercorn Marinated Chicken

8	cloves garlic, diced	8
2 Tbsp.	palm or brown sugar	30 mL
2 Tbsp.	black peppercorns, crushed	30 mL
2 Tbsp.	soy sauce	30 mL
1/4 cup	whiskey or brandy	60 mL
1 tsp.	salt	5 mL
2 1/2 lbs.	skinless boneless chicken breasts, sliced into strips about 1 inch (2.5 cm) wide	1.1 kg

This northern-style barbecued chicken dish uses local Mekong whiskey. It is often made with a whole chicken or chicken legs.

Mix the garlic, sugar, peppercorns, soy sauce, whiskey or brandy and salt together. Add the chicken and coat with the marinade. Cover and refrigerate for 3 hours or up to overnight.

Place the chicken on a baking sheet and broil in the oven or on a barbecue for 10 minutes, or until tender.

Serve it with Sweet Chili Sauce (page 22).

Serves 6.

Spicy Cilantro Roast Chicken with Honey Lime Sauce

The chicken dish and the sauce are both low-fat items and are a great way to introduce your guests to a side of Thai cooking that is not based on rich coconut sauces. You can substitute Thai basil leaves for the cilantro, for a totally different taste. The cilantro marinade can be made in advance and refrigerated for 2 days or frozen for 2 months. It can be used to marinate chicken, pork or fish for 30 minutes before cooking.

1/4 cup	cilantro leaves and stems	60 mL
2 Tbsp.	onion, diced	30 mL
2 Tbsp.	chopped garlic	30 mL
2 tsp.	crushed black peppercorns	10 mL
4	skinless boneless chicken breasts	4
1 Tbsp.	soy sauce	15 mL
2 tsp.	water	10 mL
1/2 tsp.	salt	2.5 mL
1 recipe	Honey Lime Sauce (page 17)	1 recipe

Place the cilantro, onion, garlic and peppercorns in a food processor and purée to a paste, or pound to a paste with a mortar and pestle.

Combine the mixture with the chicken, soy sauce, water and salt. Marinate for at least 30 minutes.

Preheat the oven to 400°F (200°C). Place the chicken on a baking sheet and roast for 15 to 20 minutes, depending on the size of the breasts.

Spoon the honey lime sauce over the chicken and serve.

Serves 4.

Coconut Lemon Grass Baked Chicken

3	cloves garlic, minced	3
1/2 tsp.	black peppercorns, crushed	2.5 mL
1/4 cup	fish sauce	60 mL
2 Tbsp.	whiskey or brandy	30 mL
1 Tbsp.	Red Curry Paste (page 8)	15 mL
3 Tbsp.	finely chopped lemon grass	45 mL
3 Tbsp.	coconut milk	45 mL
1 tsp.	salt	5 mL
3 lbs.	chicken thighs	1.35 kg

This northern-style dish is very simple. The best flavor is achieved by marinating for a longer time. You can use any cut of chicken, but I find that the thighs or wings have more flavor and moisture than chicken breasts.

Combine all the ingredients except the chicken in a large bowl. Add the chicken and make sure it's well coated in the marinade. Marinate in the fridge for a minimum of 15 minutes and up to 10 hours.

Preheat the oven to 350°F (175°C).

Place the chicken on a baking sheet and bake for about 45 minutes, or until the meat is no longer pink when the thigh is sliced through to the bone.

Serve with Sweet Chili Sauce (page 22).

Serves 6.

Pineapple Chicken and Cashews in Banana Leaves (page 91)

Spicy Cilantro Roast Chicken with Honey Lime Sauce (page 101)

Seared Scallops and Basil Mango Sauce (page 85)

Herb Glazed Chicken

This dish is intended to be served as part of a larger meal. The sweet, aromatic flavor contrasts well with an assortment of curries and stir-fries.

³/₄ cup	palm or brown sugar	180 mL
3 Tbsp.	fish sauce	45 mL
¹/₂ cup	water	120 mL
1 tsp.	Szechuan peppercorns	5 mL
2 Tbsp.	chopped cilantro stems	30 mL
2	cloves garlic, crushed	2
2 lbs.	skinless boneless chicken breasts, cut in cubes	900 g
1 cup	diced red bell pepper	240 mL
¹/₄ cup	sliced Thai basil or cilantro leaves	60 mL

Place the sugar, fish sauce and water in a wok over high heat and cook until the sugar is dissolved.

Toast the peppercorns in a dry pan over high heat for a minute or two. Crush them in a mortar and pestle.

Add the cilantro stems, garlic and crushed peppercorns to the wok and continue cooking until the liquid is slightly reduced.

Add the chicken and simmer over medium heat until it is cooked through and glazed in the caramelized sauce, 3 to 5 minutes. Add the red pepper and cook for 1 more minute.

Stir in the basil or cilantro leaves just before serving.

Serves 4 to 6.

Chicken and Mushrooms in Green Coconut Curry

4 tsp.	oil	20 mL
1	large onion, sliced in wedges	1
1	large green bell pepper, sliced in 2-inch (2.5-cm) pieces	1
1 cup	sliced button mushrooms	240 mL
1 cup	sliced shiitake mushrooms	240 mL
4–6 Tbsp.	Green Curry Paste (page 9)	60–90 mL
4 cups	coconut milk	950 mL
2 Tbsp.	fish sauce	30 mL
2 Tbsp.	palm or brown sugar	30 mL
1 lb.	skinless boneless chicken cut in 1-inch (2.5-cm) cubes	455 g
5	sliced kaffir lime leaves	5
1/2 cup	Thai basil leaves	120 mL

Green curry paste gives this dish the fresh flavor of raw peppers. Most types of mushrooms would be good in this curry; I like the different flavors of fresh and dried shiitake mushrooms. Sliced Chinese eggplant is often added to a green curry.

Heat 2 tsp. (10 mL) of the oil in a wok over high heat. Add the onion and green pepper and fry until the onion softens. Add the mushrooms and sauté for another 2 minutes on high heat. Remove the vegetables and set them aside.

Heat the remaining 2 tsp. (10 mL) oil in the same wok over medium heat. Fry the curry paste for about 2 minutes. Add the coconut milk and bring to a boil. Let the sauce boil for 2 to 3 minutes, then add the fish sauce and sugar.

Add the sautéed vegetables, chicken and lime leaves to the sauce. Simmer until the chicken is cooked, about 10 minutes. Chop the basil and add it to the sauce just before serving.

Serves 4.

Coconut Curry Chicken with Ginger and Eggplant

This dish is different from most Thai curries because there is no cumin, coriander or turmeric in the spice paste. The three additions of ginger also give it a special flavor. Chicken thighs give the dish a deeper flavor, but chicken breasts will work.

Pound the spice paste ingredients together using a mortar and pestle, or purée all the ingredients in a blender or food processor. Use a little water if necessary to make a paste. This will make about $^1/_2$ cup (120 mL) of paste. The unused portion can be refrigerated for a week or frozen for 2 months. It can be used to flavor any coconut curry.

To prepare the dish, place 1 cup (240 mL) of the coconut milk in a wok and bring it to a boil. Continue cooking and stirring until it separates, 3 to 5 minutes. Add 1 Tbsp. (15 mL) of the ginger and $^1/_4$ cup (60 mL) of the spice paste and boil for a couple of minutes. Add another 1 Tbsp. (15 mL) of the ginger and the sugar and boil for another couple of minutes.

Stir in the fish sauce, the last 1 Tbsp. (15 mL) of ginger and the chicken. Simmer until the chicken is cooked, stirring occasionally, about 15 minutes.

Add the remaining $1^1/_2$ cups (360 mL) coconut milk and the eggplant, beans and lime leaves. Bring to a boil and simmer for 5 minutes. Stir in the basil just before serving.

Serves 4 to 6.

For the spice paste:

6	large dried red chilies	6
1	stalk lemon grass, chopped	1
1 tsp.	chopped galanga	5 mL
4	cloves garlic, chopped	4
4	shallots, chopped	4
2 Tbsp.	chopped cilantro stems	30 mL
1 tsp.	lime zest	5 mL
1 tsp.	shrimp paste	5 mL
1 tsp.	salt	5 mL
10	white peppercorns	10

For the coconut curry chicken:

$2^1/_2$ cups	coconut milk	600 mL
3 Tbsp.	julienned fresh ginger	45 mL
1 Tbsp.	palm or brown sugar	15 mL
3 Tbsp.	fish sauce	45 mL
1 lb.	skinless boneless chicken thighs or breasts, diced in small pieces	455 g
1	Chinese or Japanese eggplant, thinly sliced	1
1 cup	sliced green beans	240 mL
4	kaffir lime leaves, finely sliced	4
10	Thai basil leaves, sliced	10

Peanut Sesame Orange Chicken

2 Tbsp.	soy sauce	30 mL
1 cup	orange juice	240 mL
1 Tbsp.	sugar	15 mL
1 tsp.	hot sauce	5 mL
2 tsp.	cornstarch	10 mL
3 Tbsp.	vegetable oil	45 mL
1	onion, sliced	1
1	red bell pepper, sliced	1
1 1/2 cups	broccoli florets	360 mL
2 Tbsp.	sesame oil	30 mL
1 lb.	skinless boneless chicken breasts, sliced in thin strips	455 g
1 cup	baby corn	240 mL
2 Tbsp.	sesame seeds	30 mL
1/2 cup	chopped roasted peanuts	120 mL

> This dish has a light, fresh flavor and nicely balances a richer curried vegetable dish.

Mix the soy sauce, orange juice, sugar, hot sauce and cornstarch together in a small bowl and set aside.

Heat 1 Tbsp. (15 mL) of the vegetable oil in a wok over high heat. Add the onion, red pepper and broccoli and stir-fry until the broccoli is tender but still a little crisp. Remove and keep warm.

Add the remaining 2 Tbsp. (30 mL) vegetable oil and the sesame oil to the wok. When it's hot, add the chicken and stir-fry until it's browned, 4 to 5 minutes.

Return the vegetables to the wok, add the baby corn and pour in the orange juice mixture. Bring to a boil, stirring constantly. Add the sesame seeds and peanuts. Cook for 2 more minutes on medium heat.

Serves 4.

Vegetables

Vegetables in Lemon Grass Broth

1 cup	Lemon Grass Broth (page 26)	240 mL
1 tsp.	white sugar	5 mL
1 tsp.	soy sauce	5 mL
1 tsp.	lime juice	5 mL
2 cups	assorted sliced vegetables (beans, carrots, etc.)	475 mL

This great, low-fat cooking method gives a subtle citrus taste to any vegetable you cook in the broth. Broccoli, cauliflower and squash all take on a tremendous flavor when simmered this way.

Heat the broth in a saucepan until it reaches a boil.

Add the sugar, soy sauce and lime juice. Add the vegetables, starting with the harder ones that need longer cooking. Cook until tender, adding more broth if needed.

Serves 4.

Mushroom Satay

I learned this recipe from my friend Kay Leong, a food consultant who is an expert in the use of Asian ingredients. I like the idea of cutting the mushrooms into a spiral shape instead of just sticking them on the skewers. I have used portobello and crimini mushrooms in this dish—use whatever type you have on hand. Serve with a peanut sauce (pages 13 to 16) and Cucumber Chili Salad (page 69).

1 Tbsp.	chopped lemon grass	15 mL
1 tsp.	chopped galanga	5 mL
2 Tbsp.	chopped cilantro stems	30 mL
2	cloves garlic, chopped	2
1/2 tsp.	ground black pepper	2.5 mL
2 Tbsp.	curry powder	30 mL
1 Tbsp.	palm or brown sugar	15 mL
1/4 tsp.	salt	1.2 mL
2 1/2 cups	large fresh shiitake mushrooms, stemmed	600 mL
1/2 cup	coconut milk	120 mL

Combine the lemon grass, galanga, cilantro, garlic, pepper, curry powder, sugar and salt. Pound to a paste with a mortar and pestle or purée in a food processor.

To cut the mushrooms into a spiral, place them gill side down on a cutting board. Place the tip of a small sharp knife in the center and cut a spiral bull's-eye pattern. You will now be able to unwind the mushroom into a long strip.

Place the paste in a large bowl and stir in the coconut milk. Add the mushrooms and marinate for about 30 minutes.

Thread the mushrooms onto skewers and broil or grill for 3 to 4 minutes, turning occasionally.

Serves 4.

Rachini's Mushroom Stir-fry

2 Tbsp.	oil	30 mL
2 cups	button mushrooms, thickly sliced	475 mL
2	cloves garlic, chopped	2
1 cup	straw mushrooms (canned)	240 mL
1 cup	fresh shiitake mushrooms, sliced (or dried and reconstituted)	240 mL
2 Tbsp.	Maggi seasoning sauce	30 mL
6	green onions, cut in 2-inch (5-cm) chunks	6

This is another example of a mild-tasting, simple vegetable accompaniment intended to contrast with other dishes in a spicy meal. I first had this stir-fry while visiting my friend Sanit's mother in her home on the outskirts of a little village several hours north of Bangkok. Everyone took part in making different dishes and Rachini, a shy family friend, made these mushrooms.

Heat the oil in a wok over high heat. Add the button mushrooms and garlic and sauté them for about 2 minutes.

Add the straw and shiitake mushrooms, Maggi seasoning sauce and green onion, and sauté for another 2 minutes.

Serves 4.

Eggplant Stuffed with Coconut and Cilantro

These eggplant morsels could be served as an appetizer or a side dish. They can be made ahead of time and reheated in the oven. I often make this with zucchini instead of eggplant.

In a bowl, thoroughly combine the coconut, cilantro, lime juice, curry paste, fish sauce and sugar.

Slice the eggplant into 2-inch (5-cm) rounds. Make two $^1/_2$-inch-deep (1.2-cm) slits diagonally across each round to form an X. Pry them apart and stuff the slits in the eggplant with the coconut mixture.

Heat the oil and water over high heat in a frying pan. Place the stuffed eggplant in the pan and cook covered for 8 to 10 minutes, depending on the desired texture.

Serves 4.

1 cup	dried shredded coconut	240 mL
$^1/_2$ cup	chopped cilantro	120 mL
2 tsp.	lime juice	10 mL
1 tsp.	Green Curry Paste (page 9)	5 mL
1 tsp.	fish sauce	5 mL
1 tsp.	palm or brown sugar	5 mL
2	Chinese or Japanese eggplants	2
1 Tbsp.	oil	15 mL
1 cup	water	240 mL

Eggplant and Potato in
Green Coconut Curry Sauce

3 Tbsp.	oil	45 mL
1	large onion, sliced in wedges	1
4	Chinese or Japanese eggplants, sliced in 1-inch (2.5-cm) pieces	4
4 Tbsp.	Green Curry Paste (page 9)	60 mL
4 cups	coconut milk	950 mL
2 tsp.	palm or brown sugar	10 mL
3 Tbsp.	fish sauce or soy sauce	45 mL
2 cups	diced cooked potatoes	475 mL
4	kaffir lime leaves, sliced	4
1/2 cup	sliced Thai basil leaves	120 mL

There are many types of eggplant in Thailand that are not usually seen in the West. One is green and the size of a grape, with a thick skin and a slightly bitter flavor. Another is pale green with white markings. It is the size of a lime, has lots of seeds and a very mild flavor. This curry dish would usually be made with an assortment of different eggplants.

Heat 2 Tbsp. (30 mL) of the oil in a wok over high heat. Add the onion and sauté for about 3 minutes. Add the eggplant and cook until it is a little soft. Remove with a slotted spoon and set aside.

In the same wok, heat the remaining oil over medium heat. Add the curry paste and fry for 2 minutes.

Add the coconut milk and bring to a boil. Lower the temperature to medium and cook for 5 minutes. Add the sugar and the fish sauce or soy sauce.

Add the sautéed vegetables, potatoes and lime leaves. Cook for 10 minutes, then add the basil. Serve with rice.

Serves 4.

Stir-fried Spinach with Salted Soybeans

Several varieties of spinach grow in Thailand. One has large thick leaves that hold up well when cooked. Unless your produce market is very resourceful, you may never see this for sale in the West, but common spinach will do nicely in this recipe. Bottled salted soybeans are available in most Asian markets. Chinese black bean and garlic sauce would be a good substitute.

2	cloves garlic, minced	2
2–5	small fresh red chilies, chopped	2–5
1 Tbsp.	salted soybeans	15 mL
1 Tbsp.	oyster sauce	15 mL
1 tsp.	white sugar	15 mL
4	bunches spinach, leaves only, washed and coarsely cut	4
10	Thai basil leaves	10
2 Tbsp.	oil	30 mL

Mix the garlic, chilies, salted soybeans, oyster sauce, sugar, spinach and basil together.

Heat the oil in a wok until it's smoking. Add the spinach mixture and stir-fry until it's warm.

Serves 4.

Curried Spinach with Tofu and Cashews

4	bunches spinach, leaves only, washed and coarsely cut	4
3 Tbsp.	oil	45 mL
2 cups	diced extra-firm tofu	475 mL
1	large onion, sliced	1
2	green bell peppers, sliced in small wedges	2
4 Tbsp.	Green Curry Paste (page 9)	60 mL
3 cups	chicken or vegetable stock	720 mL
2 tsp.	palm or brown sugar	10 mL
3 Tbsp.	fish sauce or soy sauce	45 mL
1 cup	toasted cashews	240 mL
4	kaffir lime leaves, sliced	4
1/2 cup	sliced Thai basil leaves	120 mL

This dish can be either a side dish or a vegetarian main course. For a very luxurious, rich-tasting sauce, substitute coconut milk for the stock.

Bring 8 cups (2 L) of water to a boil in a large pot. Add the spinach and cook for 1 minute. Drain the spinach and rinse under cold water. Drain again and set aside.

Heat 2 Tbsp. (30 mL) of the oil in a wok over high heat. Add the tofu and sauté until it's lightly browned. Remove with a slotted spoon and set aside. Add the onion and green pepper and sauté for about 3 minutes. Remove and set aside.

Heat the remaining oil in the wok over medium heat. Add the curry paste and fry for 2 minutes.

Add the stock and bring to a boil. Lower the temperature to medium. Cook for 5 minutes. Add the sugar and fish sauce or soy sauce. Add the tofu, spinach, sautéed vegetables, cashews and lime leaves. Cook for 5 to 10 minutes, then add the basil. Serve with rice.

Serves 4 to 6.

Chili Garlic Beans with Cashews

The beans most frequently used in Thailand are snake beans, also known as yard-long beans (*dow gok* in Chinese markets). They have a nice crisp texture and taste a little like a combination of green bean and asparagus. Fresh common green beans are a good substitute. Cashew trees grow in vast profusion in the south of Thailand, so cashews are inexpensive and plentiful in the markets. The dried chilies are meant to be cooked whole so they can give a subtle chili flavor to the other ingredients.

3 Tbsp.	oil	45 mL
3/4 cup	cashews	180 mL
2	onions, diced	2
4	cloves garlic, coarsely chopped	4
2 Tbsp.	small whole dried chilies	30 mL
1 1/2 lbs.	long beans or green beans, sliced in 3-inch (7.5-cm) pieces	680 g
1/2 cup	water or stock	120 mL
2 Tbsp.	soy sauce	30 mL
2 Tbsp.	white sugar	30 mL

Heat the oil in a wok over high heat and fry the cashews until lightly browned. Remove from the wok with a slotted spoon and set aside to drain on a paper towel.

Add the onion and fry for 1 minute. Add the garlic, chilies and beans. Stir-fry on high heat for 1 to 2 minutes.

Add the water or stock and cook until the beans are tender, about 2 more minutes.

Add the soy sauce and sugar and cook for another minute. Stir in the cashews just before serving.

Serves 4.

Coconut-Lime Green Beans and Bamboo Shoots

2 cups	green beans, sliced in 2-inch (5-cm) pieces	475 mL
1 cup	coconut milk	240 mL
1/4 cup	crispy fried shallots	60 mL
1/4 cup	crispy fried garlic	60 mL
1 tsp.	hot sauce	5 mL
1 Tbsp.	palm or brown sugar	15 mL
1/2	lime, juiced	1/2
1/4 cup	cilantro leaves	60 mL
1 Tbsp.	oil	15 mL
2 Tbsp.	chopped fresh ginger	30 mL
2 cups	bamboo shoots, sliced in thin strips	475 mL

Bamboo can grow almost a foot (30 cm) a day in the tropics, so it is a plentiful, inexpensive food that is cooked in many different ways. In the West, bamboo shoots are usually available canned and should be rinsed well in hot water after being removed from the can. You can use either long beans or common green beans in this dish. I sometimes make a lower-fat version using chicken stock instead of coconut milk. When asparagus is in season, I substitute asparagus tips for the beans.

Bring 8 cups (2 L) water to a boil in a large pot. Add the beans and cook for 1 minute. Drain the beans and rinse under cold water. Drain again and set aside.

Combine the coconut milk, shallots, garlic, hot sauce, sugar and lime juice in a saucepan. Bring to a boil. Add the cilantro. Purée the mixture in a blender. Set the sauce aside.

Heat the oil over medium heat. Add the ginger, beans and bamboo shoots and stir-fry until they're warm. Add the sauce and cook for 1 minute.

Serves 4.

Stir-fried Red Curry Mango Vegetables

This dish has only a hint of the flavor of red curry paste, which contrasts well with the sweet taste of the mango. Do not restrict yourself to the vegetables listed; this is a great recipe to help you clear out your refrigerator.

Heat the oil in a wok over high heat. Add the onion and sauté until soft. Add the garlic, zucchini, bok choy, peppers and carrot. Stir-fry until the vegetables are tender.

Add the curry paste and stir-fry for 1 minute.

Mix in all the other ingredients and cook for 1 or 2 minutes.

Serves 4.

2 Tbsp.	oil	30 mL
1	onion, sliced in small wedges	1
2	cloves garlic, diced	2
2	zucchinis, sliced into matchsticks	2
2 cups	bok choy or sui choy, thinly sliced	475 mL
1	red bell pepper, sliced in small wedges	1
1	green bell pepper, sliced in small wedges	1
1	carrot, very thinly sliced	1
2 Tbsp.	Red Curry Paste (page 8)	30 mL
2 cups	mung bean sprouts	475 mL
1	ripe mango, peeled and diced	1
1 Tbsp.	palm or brown sugar	15 mL
2 Tbsp.	soy sauce or fish sauce	30 mL
3/4 cup	chicken or vegetable stock	180 mL
1/2 cup	sliced Thai basil leaves	120 mL

Curried Vegetables in Banana Leaves

1/2 cup	coconut cream (the thick top portion of canned coconut milk)	120 mL
1 Tbsp.	Green Curry Paste (page 9)	15 mL
1 tsp.	palm or brown sugar	5 mL
1 Tbsp.	lime zest	15 mL
2 Tbsp.	chopped cilantro leaves	30 mL
2 Tbsp.	chopped mint leaves	30 mL
	salt and ground black pepper to taste	
2 cups	assorted sliced vegetables (green beans, carrots, eggplant, etc.)	475 mL
2	12-inch (30-cm) frozen banana leaves, defrosted (see page 153)	2

These banana-leaf packages can be made the night before and refrigerated until you are ready to cook them. This is the same as marinating, and the taste from the flavoring agents will be stronger. If you cook these packages on a barbecue, use a medium heat and close the lid on the barbecue. If you can't get banana leaves, use aluminum foil or parchment paper.

Preheat the oven to 400°F (200°C).

Mix the coconut cream, curry paste, sugar, lime zest, cilantro, mint and salt and pepper together. Toss the vegetables in the mixture.

Place 1 cup (240 mL) of the coated vegetables on a banana leaf. Fold the leaf to completely enclose the vegetables. Pin together with toothpicks. Repeat with the second banana leaf. Place the banana leaf packages on a baking sheet.

Place in the oven and bake for 20 minutes, or grill on a barbecue for about 15 minutes.

Serves 4.

Bean Sprout and Scallion Stir-fry

Most Thai meals have a variety of curries and spicy dishes. A simple vegetable stir-fry like this is included to cool the palate.

2 Tbsp.	oil	30 mL
2	cloves garlic, chopped	2
6 cups	mung bean sprouts	1.5 L
1 cup	chopped green onions	240 mL
2 Tbsp.	sesame oil	30 mL
2 Tbsp.	oyster sauce	30 mL
1 Tbsp.	fish sauce	15 mL
2 Tbsp.	lime juice	30 mL

Heat the oil in a wok over medium heat. Add the garlic and stir-fry until cooked but not brown. Raise the heat to high, add the bean sprouts and stir-fry for 1 minute. Add the green onions, sesame oil, oyster sauce, fish sauce and lime juice. Cook for another 30 seconds and serve immediately.

Serves 4.

Thai Basil and Sweet Corn

8	cloves garlic, coarsely chopped	8
4	small chilies	4
¹/₄ cup	cilantro stems	60 mL
¹/₄ cup	fish sauce or soy sauce	60 mL
2 Tbsp.	oil	30 mL
4 cups	corn kernels	950 mL
2 Tbsp.	palm or brown sugar	30 mL
1 cup	Thai basil leaves	240 mL

Corn was introduced to Thailand from the West and has become a very popular food. On my latest visit, I had fantastic, sweet-tasting, grilled corn on the cob from a vendor on the streets of Bangkok's Chinatown. This dish is best with fresh kernels cut off the cob, but frozen corn will work.

Pound the garlic, chilies, cilantro and fish sauce or soy sauce to a paste in a mortar and pestle. Set aside.

Heat the oil in a wok over medium heat. Add the garlic paste and fry for 1 minute, stirring constantly. Add the corn and sugar. Fry, stirring, until the corn is warm. Add the basil and serve immediately.

Serves 4.

Rice and
Noodles

Jasmine Rice

2 cups	jasmine rice	475 mL
3 cups	water	720 mL
1 tsp.	salt	5 mL

Jasmine rice is the most popular rice in Thailand. It is a high-quality long-grain white rice with a mild floral scent to it, hence its name. Rice is the base of almost every meal in Thailand. Curries, sauces and soups are often seen as just things to flavor rice with.

Wash the rice three times in cold water and then drain.

Place the rice in a heavy pot and add the water and salt. Bring to a boil. Cover the pot and lower the heat to a simmer. Cook for 20 minutes. Fluff with a fork and serve.

Makes 4 cups (950 mL).

Thai Black or Red Rice

1 cup	black or red rice	240 mL
2 cups	cold water	475 mL
1 tsp.	salt	5 mL

Black rice is a glutinous or sticky rice with a very hearty flavor. It is used throughout Southeast Asia to make rice pudding. In the north of Thailand it is served along with savory dishes like curries. Red rice is hard rice, a little bit like the brown rice found in Western markets and health food stores. The flavor is complex and nutty. It goes well with all types of curry.

Wash the rice three times in cold water and then drain.

Place the rice in a heavy pot and add the water and salt. Bring to a boil. Cover the pot and lower the heat to a simmer. Cook for about 45 minutes, or until the rice is tender.

Makes 2 cups (475 mL).

Ginger-Infused Toasted Coconut Jasmine Rice

This is an easy way to get a very flavorful rice dish. The slow simmering of the water gradually infuses the rice with the taste and aroma of the ginger and coconut. Use untoasted shredded coconut for a more subtle flavor.

2 cups	jasmine rice	475 mL
3 cups	water	720 mL
1/2 cup	toasted sweetened shredded coconut	120 mL
1 Tbsp.	chopped fresh ginger	15 mL
1 tsp.	salt	5 mL

Wash the rice in cold water three times and drain well. Place the rice in a heavy pot and add the water, toasted coconut, ginger and salt.

Bring the rice to a boil. Cover the pot and lower the heat to a simmer. Cook for 20 minutes. Fluff with a fork and serve.

Serves 4.

How to Toast Coconut

Spread the coconut out on a cookie sheet and bake at 350°F (175°C) for 5 minutes, or until lightly browned.

Lemon Grass Risotto

1¹/₂ Tbsp.	butter	22.5 mL
1¹/₂ Tbsp.	vegetable oil	22.5 mL
1 cup	finely diced onion	240 mL
3	stalks lemon grass, minced	3
1 tsp.	chopped fresh ginger	5 mL
1¹/₂ cups	short-grain Japanese or Arborio rice	360 mL
6–8 cups	Thai Chicken Stock (page 25)	1.5–2 L
¹/₄ cup	Parmesan cheese	60 mL
1 cup	dry white wine	240 mL

This is a fusion of Italian and Thai ingredients and technique. Risotto requires constant stirring and should be made just before serving. The subtle flavor of the lemon grass and ginger are infused into the rice by the long cooking process. The texture of the rice becomes creamy but it should still have a little firmness to it. This dish is heavenly when served with roast duck and Vegetables in Lemon Grass Broth (page 108).

Heat the butter and oil in a heavy pan over medium heat. Add the onion and sauté until soft. Add the lemon grass and ginger and sauté for 1 more minute. Add the rice and continue to cook, stirring, for about 3 minutes.

In another saucepan bring the stock to a simmer. Ladle 1 cup (240 mL) of the stock into the rice, continuing to stir constantly. When the stock is absorbed, add another cupful (240 mL) of stock. Continue adding the stock ¹/₂ cup (120 mL) at a time, stirring constantly, until the rice is creamy and cooked to a slightly chewy texture. Add the cheese and wine and cook for 1 more minute.

Serves 4.

Pineapple Fried Rice

This is a spectacular presentation if served in the pineapple shell; however, you can use canned pineapple if a fresh one is not available. It may be necessary to adjust the sugar, depending on how ripe or tart the pineapple is. If you cannot find wood ear mushrooms, substitute reconstituted dried shiitake mushrooms.

1	large fresh pineapple	1
1/4 cup	vegetable oil	60 mL
1	medium onion, chopped	1
2	cloves garlic, diced	2
1 cup	presoaked, sliced wood ear mushrooms	240 mL
4 cups	cooked, cooled jasmine rice (see page 122)	950 mL
6 Tbsp.	fish sauce	90 mL
1 Tbsp.	sugar	15 mL
1/2 tsp.	ground white pepper	2.5 mL
2	green onions, sliced	2
1/4 cup	sliced cilantro	60 mL

Cut the pineapple in half and hollow out the shells. Cube the pineapple flesh.

Heat the oil in a wok over high heat and stir-fry the onion until soft. Add the garlic and stir-fry for 30 seconds. With the heat on high, add the mushrooms, pineapple, rice, fish sauce, sugar and pepper.

Mix thoroughly and cook until heated through. Add the green onions and cilantro.

Serve in the hollowed-out pineapple shell.

Serves 4 to 6.

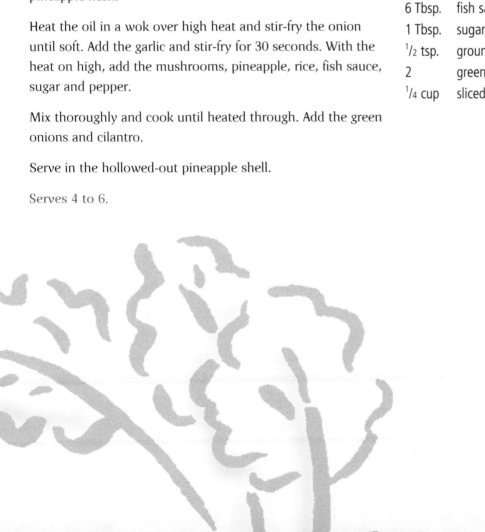

Chicken and Cashew Fried Rice

¹/₄ cup	vegetable oil	60 mL
2	cloves garlic, minced	2
1 cup	chopped onions	240 mL
2 cups	diced boneless, skinless chicken	475 mL
1¹/₃ cups	sliced shiitake mushrooms	320 mL
4 cups	cooked, cooled jasmine rice (see page 122)	950 mL
4	eggs, beaten	4
3 Tbsp.	fish sauce	45 mL
1 tsp.	Roasted Chili Paste (page 12)	5 mL
¹/₂ tsp.	ground black pepper	2.5 mL
1 cup	toasted cashews	240 mL
8	green onions, chopped	8
¹/₄ cup	cilantro leaves	60 mL
8	thin lime wedges	8

It is essential to use rice that has been cooled when making fried rice. Traditionally, it would be leftover rice from a previous meal. Fresh hot rice would stick to the wok and turn to mush.

Heat the oil in a wok over high heat. Add the garlic and fry for 10 seconds. Add the onion, chicken and mushrooms and fry for 2 minutes, or until the chicken is no longer pink.

Add the rice and continue to stir-fry on high heat until it is warm, 1 to 2 minutes. Stir in the beaten egg and cook until set. Stir in the fish sauce, chili paste and pepper.

Stir in the cashews and remove from the heat. Sprinkle the green onions and cilantro on top just before serving. Garnish with the lime wedges.

Serves 4.

Tiger Prawn and Basil Fried Rice

Fried rice plays a big role in Thai families, where it is served frequently as a one-dish meal. It is an adaptable and practical dish that is usually based on leftovers, and with a little imagination and a few basic techniques, an infinite variety is possible.

Slice the prawns in half, lengthwise. Heat the oil in a wok over high heat and fry the garlic and chili until the garlic is fragrant, less than a minute.

Add the prawn halves and stir-fry for 15 seconds over high heat.

Add the sugar, soy sauce and fish sauce. Stir thoroughly and add the basil leaves. Add the rice and stir-fry on high heat until it's hot.

Serve on a platter surrounded by cucumber slices.

Serves 4.

12	tiger prawns, medium size, shelled	12
1/4 cup	vegetable oil	60 mL
2 tsp.	chopped garlic	10 mL
1 tsp.	diced fresh red chilies	5 mL
1 tsp.	sugar	5 mL
2 tsp.	dark soy sauce	10 mL
1 Tbsp.	fish sauce	15 mL
1/2 cup	sliced Thai basil leaves	120 mL
2 cups	cooked, cooled jasmine rice (see page 122)	475 mL
1	long English cucumber, thinly sliced	1

Ginger and Mushroom Baked Coconut Rice

1 Tbsp.	oil	15 mL
1	onion, diced	1
1 Tbsp.	finely chopped fresh ginger	15 mL
1 cup	sliced mushrooms	240 mL
1	red chili, chopped	1
1	green onion, sliced	1
1 tsp.	soy sauce	5 mL
1 Tbsp.	oyster sauce	15 mL
¼ cup	toasted coconut (see page 123)	60 mL
2 cups	cooked, cooled jasmine rice (see page 122)	475 mL

This is an easy dish to make ahead of time. It can be assembled the night before you need it and then the next day you can just pop it in the oven. This leaves your stove burners free to stir-fry up a storm of tasty accompaniments.

Heat the oil in a wok or a skillet over high heat and fry the onion, ginger, mushrooms and chili together for about 2 minutes. Add the green onion, soy sauce and oyster sauce to the mushroom mixture. Add this mixture and the coconut to the rice and stir to mix.

Preheat the oven to 375°F (190°C). Place the rice mixture in an oiled 4-cup (1-L) casserole and bake covered for 10 to 15 minutes.

Serves 2 to 4.

Egg Noodles with Thai Herb Pesto

The technique used to make this herb paste is very similar to an Italian pesto. The flavors are multi-layered and fresh. Try changing the proportions of the chili, ginger and mint in the herb paste to bring up the flavor of these ingredients. Every time you change it, you will taste a different aspect of the dish.

1/2 cup	vegetable oil	120 mL
2 Tbsp.	raw peanuts	30 mL
1	small green chili, diced	1
1	3/4-inch (2-cm) piece galanga, finely chopped	1
2	cloves garlic, finely diced	2
1 cup	Thai basil leaves	240 mL
3/4 cup	cilantro leaves	180 mL
1/4 cup	mint leaves	60 mL
2 Tbsp.	lime juice	30 mL
2 tsp.	fish sauce	10 mL
12 oz.	thin fresh egg noodles	340 g

Heat the oil in a pan over high heat. Add the peanuts and stir-fry for about 1 minute, or until browned. Remove the nuts with a slotted spoon and drain on a paper towel. Reserve the oil.

Put water on to boil for the noodles.

In a food processor, grind the peanuts, then add the chili, galanga and garlic. Mix briefly, and add the basil, cilantro, mint, lime juice, fish sauce and the oil saved from frying the peanuts. Mix briefly to combine.

Boil the noodles for about 2 minutes, drain and toss the hot noodles in the herb sauce. Serve hot.

Serves 4.

Chiang Mai Noodles

7 oz.	fresh egg noodles	200 g
1/2 cup	vegetable oil	120 mL
1	large onion, finely sliced	1
6	large cloves garlic, finely sliced	6
2 Tbsp.	Red Curry Paste (page 8)	30 mL
1 lb.	boneless pork or chicken, finely diced	455 g
3 Tbsp.	fish sauce	45 mL
2 Tbsp.	palm or brown sugar	30 mL
1/4 cup	sliced cilantro	60 mL
1/4 cup	finely sliced green onions	60 mL
1/2	lime, juiced	1/2
	whole cilantro leaves, for garnish	

Chiang Mai is a city in northern Thailand that has become well known as a center for organizing elephant treks through the mountain regions. We traveled by *tuk tuk*, a three-wheeled motorcycle taxi, 200 bumpy miles (320 kilometers) north into the mountains to visit a village where the people dyed fabric with indigo plants and then embroidered incredible designs before turning it into clothing. This is what we had for lunch at a roadside stand outside the village.

Cook the noodles in boiling water until tender, about 2 minutes. Drain and set aside.

Heat 1/4 cup (60 mL) of the oil in a wok until it's hot. Add the onion and fry until golden. Remove with a slotted spoon and set aside to drain on a paper towel.

In the same oil, fry the garlic until it's crisp and golden; remove and set aside.

Add the remaining 1/4 cup (60 mL) oil to the wok and stir-fry the curry paste for 1 minute. Add the pork or chicken, fish sauce and sugar to the curry paste. Stir-fry for several minutes on high heat.

Add the cooked noodles to the meat mixture and toss together to warm the noodles. Add the cilantro, green onions and lime juice. Garnish with the fried onions and garlic and a few cilantro leaves.

Serves 4.

Shiitake Mushroom Rice Noodle Stir-fry

The shiitake mushrooms and oyster sauce give this dish a rich taste that contrasts well with a spicy curry.

Soak the noodles in tepid water for 10 to 15 minutes, then drain (see page 132). Set aside.

Remove the stems from the mushrooms and discard them. Slice the mushrooms. Set aside.

In a small bowl, stir together the fish sauce, stock, oyster sauce, sugar, paprika and hot sauce. Set aside.

Heat the oil in a wok over high heat. Add the onion and fry until browned. Add the garlic and sauté for 30 seconds. Push the onion and garlic to the sides of the wok.

Add the drained noodles and mushrooms to the wok and stir-fry at a high temperature for 1 to 2 minutes, adding a little stock or water to the wok if necessary to keep the noodles from sticking.

Add the stock mixture and cook for 1 minute. Add the bean sprouts, green onions and cilantro. Cook for 1 more minute.

Garnish with lime wedges or squeeze the lime juice over the noodles.

Serves 4.

8 oz.	dry rice noodles	227 g
6–10	dried shiitake mushrooms, soaked in hot water until soft	6–10
1/4 cup	fish sauce	60 mL
3/4 cup	Thai Chicken Stock (page 25)	180 mL
1 Tbsp.	oyster sauce	15 mL
2 Tbsp.	palm or brown sugar	30 mL
1 Tbsp.	paprika	15 mL
1 Tbsp.	hot sauce	15 mL
1 tsp.	oil	5 mL
1	onion, diced	1
1	clove garlic, chopped	1
1 cup	bean sprouts	240 mL
2	green onions, sliced	2
1/4 cup	sliced cilantro	60 mL
1/2	lime	1/2

Bangkok Coconut Rice Noodles

1 lb.	dried rice noodles	455 g
1 Tbsp.	oil	15 mL
2	cloves garlic, chopped	2
2 tsp.	Red Curry Paste (page 8)	10 mL
2 Tbsp.	Chinese black bean and garlic sauce	30 mL
1¹/₂ cups	coconut milk	360 mL
2 Tbsp.	palm or brown sugar	30 mL
2 Tbsp.	lime juice	30 mL
1 tsp.	fish sauce	5 mL
2 tsp.	oil	10 mL
6 Tbsp.	chopped shallots	90 mL
1 tsp.	paprika	5 mL
¹/₂ lb.	mung bean sprouts	227 g
1	bunch green onions, sliced	1
¹/₂ cup	sliced cilantro leaves	120 mL

These noodles have a creamy rich flavor that goes well with a simple, fresh vegetable stir-fry.

Soak the rice noodles in tepid water for 15 minutes. Drain and set aside.

In a saucepan, heat the 1 Tbsp. (15 mL) oil over high heat. Add the garlic and curry paste and fry for about 1 minute. Mash the black bean sauce into the curry paste. Add the coconut milk, sugar, lime juice and fish sauce. Simmer for 5 to 10 minutes.

Heat the 2 tsp. (10 mL) oil in a wok over high heat. Add the shallots and stir-fry until they soften. Add the drained noodles, paprika and bean sprouts and stir-fry for 1 minute. Pour in the coconut sauce and add the green onion and cilantro.

Cook until the noodles are tender, about 3 minutes.

Serves 6.

How to Prepare Rice Noodles

Rice noodles are much more delicate than wheat noodles and if they soak for too long or if the water is too hot they will start to dissolve. If the noodles are too soft they curl up, stick and get mushy in the wok. The best technique is to drain the noodles when they are still a little stiff and soften them during the cooking process by adding a few spoonfuls of water, if necessary.

Drunkard's Noodles

This dish is a popular snack in Bangkok after a night of bar-hopping. The chilies in the dish are believed to wake you up if you have had too much to drink. I think it makes a fine meal even if you are sober.

Soak the rice noodles in tepid water for 15 minutes (see page 132). Drain.

Heat the oil in a wok until it's very hot. Add the onion, garlic and chilies. Fry until the garlic is lightly browned.

Stir in the drained noodles and add the peppers, tomato, sugar, soy sauces, basil and lime leaves. Keep stirring until the peppers and noodles are al dente, about 5 minutes. Add a little water if needed to keep the noodles from sticking to the wok.

Serves 2 to 4.

4 oz.	dried rice noodles	113 g
2 Tbsp.	oil	30 mL
1	onion, cut in thin wedges	1
1	clove garlic, diced	1
4	small red chilies, chopped	4
1	small red bell pepper, thinly sliced	1
1	small green bell pepper, thinly sliced	1
1	tomato, cut in thin wedges	1
1/2 tsp.	sugar	2.5 mL
1 tsp.	dark soy sauce	5 mL
2 Tbsp.	light soy sauce	30 mL
6	basil leaves, chopped	6
4	kaffir lime leaves, thinly sliced	4

Bangkok Street Vendor Rice Noodle Stir-fry

8 oz.	dried rice noodles	227 g
2 Tbsp.	oil	30 mL
1 cup	diced extra-firm tofu	240 mL
1	clove garlic, chopped	1
2	eggs	2
2 Tbsp.	fish sauce	30 mL
1 Tbsp.	chicken stock	15 mL
1/4 cup	palm or brown sugar	60 mL
1 Tbsp.	paprika	15 mL
1 Tbsp.	hot sauce	15 mL
1 cup	bean sprouts	240 mL
1	green onion, sliced	1
1/4 cup	sliced cilantro	60 mL
1/4 cup	chopped roasted peanuts	60 mL
1	lime	1

It seems most people in Bangkok have noodles for lunch, and there are many choices. I watched a traditionally dressed, wizened Thai women cook this for me on a very hot gas flame in less than a minute. This quantity will take longer on your stove at home.

Soak the rice noodles in warm water for 10 to 15 minutes (see page 132). Drain and set aside.

Heat 1 Tbsp. (15 mL) of the oil in a wok over high heat. Add the tofu and fry until browned. Add the garlic and fry for 30 seconds. Crack the eggs into the center of the wok and scramble them quickly. Push the egg, tofu and garlic mixture to the sides of the wok.

Add the remaining 1 Tbsp. (15 mL) of the oil to the wok and then the drained noodles. Stir-fry at a high temperature for a minute or two, adding a little water or stock to the wok if necessary to keep the noodles from sticking.

Add the fish sauce, chicken stock, sugar, paprika and hot sauce. Cook for 1 minute. Add the bean sprouts, green onion, cilantro and peanuts. Cook for 1 more minute.

Garnish with lime wedges or squeeze lime juice over the noodles.

Serves 4.

Pineapple Fried Rice (page 125)

Drunkard's Noodles (page 133)

Gingered Black Rice Pudding (page 146)

Coconut Ginger Chocolate Brownies (page 149) and Banana Lime Sauté (page 141)

Dried Shrimp (or Chicken) Paad Thai

Paad Thai is one of the national dishes of Thailand. It is undoubtedly the most recognized Thai dish in the world and there are hundreds of versions. It is said that 20 percent of the 25,000 street vendors in Bangkok are selling *Paad Thai* and each one is slightly different. That gives you a lot of leeway to make your own changes. I particularly like the sweet and sour taste of this sauce. The real key to making good *Paad Thai* is not to oversoak the noodles.

1½ cups	chicken stock	360 mL
¼ cup	tamarind water (page 48)	60 mL
⅓ cup	palm or brown sugar	80 mL
2½ Tbsp.	fish sauce	40 mL
10 oz.	dried rice noodles	284 g
4 Tbsp.	vegetable oil	60 mL
4 oz.	extra-firm tofu, diced	113 g
½	onion, diced	½
1 tsp.	chopped garlic	5 mL
¼ cup	dried shrimp, chopped, or 8 oz. (227 g) skinless boneless chicken, diced	60 mL
3	eggs, lightly beaten	3
⅓ cup	chopped roasted peanuts	80 mL
1 cup	mung bean sprouts	240 mL
3	green onions, chopped	3
1 tsp.	crushed chili flakes, toasted	5 mL
2 tsp.	lime juice	10 mL

Combine the stock, tamarind water, sugar and fish sauce in a small saucepan and bring to a boil. Simmer until reduced to ¾ cup (180 mL) and set aside. This sauce can be made in advance and will keep for 2 weeks when refrigerated.

Soak the noodles in tepid water for about 15 minutes (see page 132). Drain and set aside.

Heat 1 Tbsp. (15 mL) of the oil in a wok over high heat. Add the tofu and sauté until it's slightly browned. Remove and set aside.

Add another 1 Tbsp. (15 mL) of oil to the same wok. Add the onion, garlic and dried shrimp or chicken. Cook over high heat for about 2 minutes, then move the ingredients aside. Add the egg and scramble. Remove the egg-shrimp mixture.

Heat the remaining 2 Tbsp. (30 mL) oil. Add the noodles and cook over high heat briefly, about 1 minute. Return the egg mixture to the pan. Add the peanuts, sprouts, green onions and tofu. Sauté on high heat for 1 minute, then add the sauce and chili flakes. Cook until the sauce is absorbed. Add the lime juice and serve immediately.

Serves 2 to 4.

How to Toast Chili Flakes

Place the chili flakes in a dry frying pan over medium heat. Cook, stirring constantly, for 1 or 2 minutes, until they become slightly brown and are very aromatic. Be careful not to inhale the chili fumes.

Tiger Prawn Paad Thai

¹/₄ cup	tamarind water (page 48)	60 mL
2 Tbsp.	palm or brown sugar	30 mL
1 Tbsp.	Maggi seasoning sauce	15 mL
1 tsp.	fish sauce	5 mL
1 tsp.	soy sauce	5 mL
8 oz.	dried rice noodles	227 g
2 Tbsp.	vegetable oil	30 mL
12	raw tiger prawns, medium size, shelled	12
4	cloves garlic, chopped	4
2	eggs, beaten	2
1 cup	extra-firm tofu, cut into small dice	240 mL
2 tsp.	crushed chili flakes	10 mL
2 cups	mung bean sprouts	475 mL
1 cup	green onion, sliced in 2-inch (5-cm) pieces	240 mL
¹/₂ cup	crushed roasted peanuts	120 mL

I learned this version of *Paad Thai* while I was in Bangkok at the Suan Dusit school culinary program. I was in the kitchen observing the cooks filling orders for the restaurant they run as a training facility and this seemed to be one of the most popular dishes. The tart flavor of the tamarind really goes well with the fresh prawns.

Stir the tamarind water, sugar, Maggi seasoning sauce, fish sauce and soy sauce together in a bowl. Set aside.

Soak the noodles in tepid water for 15 minutes (see page 132). Drain and set aside.

Heat the oil until it's smoking in a wok. Add the prawns and garlic and stir-fry for 15 seconds. Add the drained noodles, egg and tofu pieces. Continuing to stir, add the chili flakes, tamarind mixture, bean sprouts and green onion. Cook until the egg is set. Scatter the peanuts on top.

Serves 2 to 4.

Chicken and Snow Peas with Curry Cream Pasta

A blending of cultures right in the pan. A cook in Italy or Thailand would probably be stunned to see the ingredients listed together here, but the proof is in the tasting. These diverse flavors blend into something deliciously unique.

Cook the pasta to al dente in boiling water, according to package directions. Drain, rinse with cold water and set aside.

Heat the olive oil in a large skillet over medium heat. Add the onion and garlic, and sauté until they are light brown. Add the chicken and curry paste and stir-fry for 1 minute. Add the coconut milk, cream, sun-dried tomatoes and fish sauce. Bring to a boil. Cook for 2 minutes, then reduce the heat to low. Add the peppers and snow peas and simmer for 5 minutes.

Stir in the pine nuts, basil and salt. Add the pasta and toss with the sauce until it is warmed through.

Serves 4.

12 oz.	dried penne pasta	340 g
3 Tbsp.	olive oil	45 mL
2 Tbsp.	chopped onion	30 mL
1 Tbsp.	chopped garlic	15 mL
1 cup	diced skinless boneless chicken	240 mL
1 tsp.	Panaeng Curry Paste (page 10)	5 mL
1 cup	coconut milk	240 mL
1/2 cup	heavy cream	120 mL
1/2 cup	sliced sun-dried tomatoes	120 mL
1 Tbsp.	fish sauce	15 mL
1/2 cup	sliced red bell peppers	120 mL
1/2 cup	sliced snow peas	120 mL
1/4 cup	toasted pine nuts	60 mL
1/4 cup	chopped basil	60 mL
	salt to taste	

How to Toast Pine Nuts

To toast pine nuts, preheat the oven to 350°F (175°C). Place the pine nuts on a baking sheet. Bake for 5 minutes, or until golden brown, stirring once or twice so they brown evenly. Watch the pine nuts carefully; they can burn quickly.

Desserts

Mango Lime Sauce

2	ripe mangos, peeled and seeded, or a 16-oz. (475-mL) can, drained	2
2 Tbsp.	lime juice	30 mL
1 cup	mango juice	240 mL

I serve this sauce with cake or chocolate ginger brownies. It's also a great topping on sliced bananas.

Purée the mangos in a food processor until smooth. Add the juices and process until combined.

Makes about 2 cups (475 mL).

Banana Whiskey Cream Sauce

3	large ripe bananas, chopped	3
1 Tbsp.	honey	15 mL
1	lime, juiced	1
1 tsp.	minced fresh ginger	5 mL
1 cup	whipping cream	240 mL
1/4 tsp.	cinnamon	1.2 mL
3 Tbsp.	whiskey	45 mL

I usually serve this sauce with chocolate ginger brownies, but it also goes well with any cake and it makes a great topping for tropical fruit. Mango or orange juice could be substituted for the whiskey.

Purée the bananas, then add everything else to the blender or food processor and purée completely. Serve the same day, so it will not discolor.

Makes about 2 1/2 cups (600 mL).

Banana Lime Sauté

This dessert takes only minutes to make and it turns plain ice cream into something spectacular. There are 30 types of bananas available in Thailand, so banana desserts of all kinds are common.

Place the butter and sugar in a medium saucepan over high heat and cook until the sugar dissolves.

Add the bananas, reduce the heat to medium and cook for about 2 minutes.

Stir in the cinnamon, lime juice, lime leaves, whiskey or rum and water. Cook for another 3 minutes. Remove the lime leaves.

Serve over vanilla or coconut ice cream.

Serves 6.

1/4 cup	butter	60 mL
1/2 cup	palm or brown sugar	120 mL
6	bananas, sliced in 1-inch (2.5-cm) pieces	6
1 tsp.	cinnamon	5 mL
1/4 cup	lime juice	60 mL
6	kaffir lime leaves	6
2 Tbsp.	whiskey or rum	30 mL
1/4 cup	water	60 mL

Sticky Rice and Mango

2 cups	sticky rice (glutinous rice)	475 mL
1 cup	coconut milk	240 mL
1/2 cup	white sugar	120 mL
1/8 tsp.	salt	.5 mL
2	ripe mangos, peeled, seeded and sliced	2

This dessert signals that mangos are in season. It is immensely popular because these simple flavors complement each other beautifully. The dish relies on fresh, ripe, sweet mango, so I recommend that you do not use canned mango. Sticky rice is available at most Asian markets.

Place the rice in a bowl and cover with cold water. Soak for at least 3 hours. Drain and rinse thoroughly.

Line the bottom of a bamboo steamer with a banana leaf or cheesecloth. Place the soaked rice in the steamer. Cover the bamboo steamer and place in a wok filled with a few inches of water. Bring the water to a slow boil and allow the rice to steam for 30 minutes.

Stir the coconut milk, sugar and salt together in a saucepan. Cook, stirring, over medium heat until the sugar dissolves. Set aside.

Place the hot rice in a bowl and pour the coconut milk mixture over it. Stir until it's completely combined.

Mound the hot sweetened rice on a serving platter and smooth the surface. Allow to cool to room temperature. Surround the rice with the sliced mangos and serve.

Serves 4.

Sticky Rice and Banana Grilled in Banana Leaves

The first time I had this snack was on the white sand beach near Big Buddha Point on Samui Island in southern Thailand. It was an amazing treat for just a few pennies and I have been in love with the flavors ever since. The rice picks up essences of banana leaf and the bananas and sweetened coconut milk caramelize on the grill. If banana leaves are not available, you can make this with foil.

1 recipe	Sticky Rice (see page 142), omitting the mango	1 recipe
4	bananas	4
4	frozen 12-inch-long (30-cm) banana leaves, defrosted (see page153)	4

Heat a barbecue to medium-hot.

Lay a banana leaf out flat on a work surface. Take ¼ of the cooked rice and spread it in a 1-inch-wide (2.5-cm) strip along the leaf near the bottom end.

Peel a banana and slice it in half lengthwise. Press the 2 banana halves into the strip of rice. Roll the banana leaf up over the rice and banana so that you end up with a tight, 1-inch-wide (2.5-cm) tube. Secure the ends of the tube with toothpicks, or tie with heavy string. Repeat with the rest of the rice, bananas and banana leaves.

Place the filled tubes on the barbecue and grill, turning occasionally. Grill for about 5 minutes in total. The rice mixture is already cooked, so you are just heating the filling to caramelize it. The time will vary, depending on the temperature and type of barbecue.

Serves 4.

Tropical Trifle

4 tsp.	cornstarch	20 mL
1 cup	milk	240 mL
1 cup	coconut milk	240 mL
2	eggs	2
6 Tbsp.	white sugar	90 mL
1 tsp.	vanilla	5 mL
2 cups	fresh or canned tropical fruits, such as mango, lychee, banana, papaya	475 mL
8 slices	Banana Mango Cake (page 150)	8 slices
1/2 cup	sherry	120 mL

I took a traditional English dessert and gave it the flavor of the tropics. This is not a dessert that you will find in Thailand, but the taste would fool a native. Numerous changes are possible here, depending on the type of cake, fruit and liquor that you use.

To make the custard, place the cornstarch in a saucepan and gradually whisk in the milk. Make sure there are no lumps. Whisk in the coconut milk.

Cook over medium heat until the mixture comes to a boil, stirring constantly. Cook 1 more minute, stirring, then remove from the heat.

Beat the eggs and sugar together in a small bowl, until well blended. Stir 1/4 of the hot milk mixture into the egg mixture, whisking well. Add the warmed egg mixture to the rest of the milk, stirring constantly.

Cook over low heat until thickened, stirring constantly. Remove from the heat and add the vanilla. Cool before using.

Assemble 4 large wine goblets. In the bottom of each one, place a couple of spoonfuls of tropical fruit. Place a couple of spoonfuls of custard over the fruit. Cover the custard with a slice of cake cut to fit the shape of the goblet. Drizzle 1 Tbsp. (15 mL) of sherry over the cake. Repeat the layers, ending with the custard. Garnish with a piece of fruit.

Serves 4.

Coconut Cream Pudding

This soft, creamy dessert is very easy to make. Make sure the cornstarch and coconut milk are whisked thoroughly before heating; otherwise you will get lumps of cornstarch that will never dissolve.

3 Tbsp.	cornstarch	45 mL
2 cups	coconut milk	475 mL
1/2 cup	light brown sugar (packed)	120 mL
	pinch salt	
1/2 tsp.	vanilla extract	2.5 mL

Place the cornstarch in a medium saucepan. Gradually whisk in the coconut milk, making sure the cornstarch is completely dissolved. Stir in the sugar and salt. Cook, whisking continually, over medium heat, until the mixture thickens and comes to a boil. Boil for 1 minute.

Stir in the vanilla. Pour into 4 custard cups. Serve warm or cool.

Serves 4.

Gingered Black Rice Pudding

1 cup	black rice	240 mL
2¹/₂ cups	water	600 mL
1 Tbsp.	finely chopped fresh ginger	15 mL
²/₃ cup	palm or brown sugar	160 mL
1 cup	coconut milk	240 mL
¹/₂ cup	coconut cream (the thick top half of canned coconut milk)	120 mL
1 tsp.	icing sugar	5 mL
	pinch salt	
¹/₂ cup	diced mango	120 mL

Black rice pudding is a favorite throughout Southeast Asia. In Indonesia it is a popular breakfast item. It can be served warm or cold and thick or thin. The texture can be varied by how much or little water you use to cook the rice. Black rice is a sticky, or glutinous, rice and thickens during the cooking process, so that egg or cornstarch is not needed.

Rinse and drain the rice.

Place the rice, water and ginger in a heavy saucepan and bring to a boil. Cover, lower the heat to a simmer and cook for about 40 minutes, or until the rice is soft.

Stir in the sugar and coconut milk and simmer for another 10 minutes. Cool to room temperature and divide among 4 bowls.

Whisk together the coconut cream, icing sugar and salt. Pour a small amount over each portion of pudding. Sprinkle the diced mango on top.

Serves 4.

Banana Coconut Candy

6	ripe bananas	6
3/4 cup	coconut milk	180 mL
1/2 cup	white sugar	120 mL
1/2 cup	palm or brown sugar	120 mL
	pinch salt	
1 cup	dried, sweetened shredded coconut, toasted (see page 123)	240 mL

Peel the bananas. Purée them in a food processor with the coconut milk until creamy.

Spray a large non-stick skillet with cooking spray and cook the banana mixture over medium-high heat until it is dry, about 10 minutes.

Stir in both sugars and salt and continue to cook until the mixture caramelizes.

Cover a cookie sheet with parchment paper. Spread the mixture on the parchment to a thickness of 1 inch (2.5 cm). Sprinkle with the toasted coconut and allow to cool.

Slice into 1- or 2-inch (2.5- or 5-cm) squares before serving.

Serves 6.

Banana Ginger Squares

1¼ cups	flour	300 mL
1 tsp.	baking soda	5 mL
¼ tsp.	nutmeg	1.2 mL
½ cup	vegetable oil	120 mL
1 cup	white sugar	240 mL
2	eggs	2
2	bananas, mashed	2
1 tsp.	lime juice	5 mL
1 tsp.	vanilla	5 mL
½ cup	chopped candied ginger	120 mL
¾ cup	dried unsweetened shredded coconut	180 mL

This easy dessert is similar to what is sold on the streets in any Thai city.

Preheat the oven to 375°F (190°C).

Sift the flour, baking soda and nutmeg together. In a separate bowl, combine the oil, sugar, eggs, banana, lime juice and vanilla. Beat thoroughly.

Fold the liquid and dry ingredients together. Stir in the candied ginger.

Pour the batter into a greased 9 x 12-inch (23 x 30-cm) pan. Scatter the coconut over the top. Bake for 30 to 40 minutes, until a toothpick inserted in the middle comes out clean. Cool and cut into squares.

Makes 16 squares.

Coconut Ginger Chocolate Brownies

This is a chocolate dessert that's never seen in Thailand, but it's rich with Asian flavor elements. I like to cut the brownies into triangles, place them on individual plates and drizzle Mango Lime Sauce (page 140) and Banana Whiskey Cream Sauce (page 140) around them.

Preheat the oven to 350°F (175°C).

Melt the butter carefully on low heat, so that it melts but does not separate. Whisk the cocoa powder into the melted butter.

In a large bowl, beat the eggs until light. Beat in the sugar, then the chocolate mixture. Blend well. Sift in the flour, salt and baking powder. Beat until completely combined.

Stir in the vanilla, chocolate chips, ginger and $^1/_4$ cup (60 mL) of the coconut. Pour into a greased 8 x 8-inch (20 x 20-cm) pan. Scatter the remaining coconut on top. Bake for 30 minutes. Cool and cut into squares.

Makes 12 brownies.

$^1/_2$ cup	butter	120 mL
$^1/_2$ cup	cocoa powder, sifted	120 mL
2	eggs	2
1 cup	white sugar	240 mL
$^3/_4$ cup	flour	180 mL
$^1/_2$ tsp.	salt	2.5 mL
$^1/_2$ tsp.	baking powder	2.5 mL
1 tsp.	vanilla	5 mL
$^1/_2$ cup	chocolate chips	120 mL
2 Tbsp.	diced crystallized ginger	30 mL
$^1/_2$ cup	dried, unsweetened shredded coconut	120 mL

Banana Mango Cake

1¼ cups	flour	300 mL
1 tsp.	baking soda	5 mL
¼ tsp.	nutmeg	1.2 mL
1 cup	white sugar	240 mL
½ cup	oil	120 mL
2	eggs	2
1 tsp.	vanilla	5 mL
1 tsp.	lemon juice	5 mL
¾ cup	diced mango or pineapple	180 mL
2	mashed bananas	2
¼ cup	coconut flakes	60 mL

This is a simple variation on a banana cake. Make sure that you do not beat the ingredients, which will prevent it from rising. It is also essential to put the cake in the oven immediately after it's folded together.

Preheat the oven to 375°F (190°C). Sift the flour, baking soda and nutmeg together. Combine the sugar, oil, eggs, vanilla, lemon juice, mango or pineapple and banana in a separate bowl. Mix thoroughly.

Fold the liquid and dry ingredients together. Pour into a greased loaf pan or a greased 9 x 12-inch (23 x 30-cm) baking pan. Scatter the coconut flakes on top.

Place in the oven and bake for 35 to 45 minutes. The baking time will vary, depending on the size and shape of the pan and the accuracy of the oven. To test the cake, insert a toothpick in the center; if it comes out dry the cake is ready.

Serves 8.

Chocolate Banana Coconut Cake

This cake has the flavor of a Thai dessert but I have turned it into a chocolate cake. I cannot justify this except to say that chocolate is my favorite food. Mango sauce is a perfect match for this scrumptious cake.

Preheat the oven to 375°F (190°C).

Sift the flour, cocoa powder, baking soda and nutmeg together. Combine the sugar, oil, eggs, banana, lemon juice and vanilla in a separate bowl. Mix thoroughly.

Fold the banana mixture into the dry ingredients. Combine gently until a uniform color is achieved. Fold in the coconut.

Pour into a buttered 5 x 9-inch (12.5 x 23-cm) loaf pan. Place in the oven and bake for 35 to 50 minutes. Baking time will vary, depending on the size and shape of the pan and the accuracy of the oven. To test the cake, insert a toothpick in the center; if it comes out dry the cake is ready.

Makes 1 loaf.

1 cup	flour	240 mL
1/4 cup	cocoa powder	60 mL
1 tsp.	baking soda	5 mL
1/4 tsp.	nutmeg	1.2 mL
1 cup	white sugar	240 mL
1/2 cup	oil	120 mL
2	eggs	2
2	bananas, mashed	2
1 tsp.	lemon juice	5 mL
1 tsp.	vanilla	5 mL
1/2 cup	dried, unsweetened shredded coconut	120 mL

Mango Cream Tarts

24	small frozen tart shells (defrosted)	24
1	large ripe mango, peeled and diced	1
1 recipe	Mango Coconut Custard Filling	1 recipe
½ cup	dried, sweetened shredded coconut, toasted (see page 123)	120 mL

These tarts are a great way to finish a meal. They can be made one day before serving and are very simple if you buy frozen tart shells. Blind baking refers to the process of lining a pastry shell with foil and filling it with raw rice or beans; the weight keeps the bottom of the pastry from puffing up in the oven.

Preheat the oven to 350°F (175°C).

Place the tart shells on a baking sheet in the oven. After 5 minutes poke the bottoms of the tarts with a fork if they are puffing up. (Or blind bake the tart shells as mentioned in the introduction.) Continue to bake the tarts until they are a golden brown color, about another 10 minutes.

Place a spoonful of diced mango in the bottom of each baked tart shell. Fill each tart shell with the custard filling and sprinkle with some of the toasted coconut. Serve warm or cold.

Makes 24 tarts.

Mango Coconut Custard Filling

6 Tbsp.	cornstarch	90 mL
2 cups	mango juice	475 mL
2 cups	coconut milk	475 mL
1 cup	white sugar	240 mL
	pinch salt	
1 tsp.	vanilla extract	

Place the cornstarch in a medium saucepan. Gradually whisk in the mango juice and coconut milk, being careful not to leave lumps. Whisk in the sugar and salt. Cook, whisking continually, over medium heat until the mixture thickens and comes to a boil. Boil for 1 minute. Remove from the heat.

Stir in the vanilla. Cool slightly before pouring the custard into the tart shells. (There will be some custard left over—it's great right out of the bowl.)

Makes about 4½ cups (1 L).

Glossary of Thai Ingredients

Banana leaves: The large flexible leaves of the banana plant are used throughout Asia to wrap foods for grilling, steaming or baking. They keep the food moist and impart a subtle, herblike flavor. To use banana leaves, remove the thick central stalk, rinse the leaves well and use as is or blanch them in boiling water for a few seconds to soften them. They are often for sale in the West in the freezer section of Vietnamese, Indian or Philippine markets. Foil or parchment paper can be used instead.

Chilies: The chili pepper is found in an amazing variety of sizes, colors and flavors throughout Asia. There are more than two dozen varieties available in Southeast Asia, including finger-length chilies in red and green; medium-length plump chilies, which can be yellow, pale white, orange, green or red; and tiny bird's-eye chilies, one of the world's hottest varieties.

Chilies are commonly sold green (unripe), red (ripe) and dried. The flavor and fragrance of green and red chilies is different and can be compared to the difference in flavor between a red and green bell pepper. The green pepper has a raw vegetable flavor, while the red pepper has a more mellow, sweeter flavor.

When dried, the chili turns dark reddish-brown and has a deeper flavor than when fresh; dried chilies will also add a deeper red color to a curry than fresh chilies. Dried chilies are usually cut in small pieces and soaked in warm water until softened, then pounded to a paste before being cooked. They can also be dry-fried or roasted gently until crisp, then ground to a coarse powder and used as a condiment or seasoning.

Some or all of the seeds may be removed according to the desired degree of heat. The hot part of a chili is actually in the oil that surrounds the ribs and the seeds; when the seeds are removed, the chili is less fiery. Be careful when handling chilies. The oil that gets on your hands will remain for hours in spite of washing. I recommend not changing your contact lenses after seeding chilies!

Coconut milk: This is not the liquid inside the coconut, but is made by grating the flesh of a fresh coconut and soaking the coconut meat in hot water for 30 minutes. The resulting coconut milk is then strained through cheesecloth and canned. It is possible to soak the same coconut meat in water a second time, but this gives a much thinner, less flavorful product with less "coconut cream" on top. This is the reason for flavor variations in different brands.

Coriander: Also known as cilantro or Chinese parsley, all parts of this plant are used in Thai cuisine. The leaves are used in dressings or as garnish. They are also added at the end of stir-fry dishes, as the flavor disappears quickly when exposed to heat. The stems and roots maintain their flavor when cooked and are used in flavoring pastes.

Crispy fried shallots or garlic: This is a commercially made product that is available in most Asian markets, sometimes labeled as fried onion. It is a popular garnish and is used as an ingredient in many salads. The texture is dry and crunchy like a potato chip, and it has a rich, caramelized taste.

Fish sauce: This is a pale amber liquid derived from a brew of anchovy-like fish or shrimp mixed with salt. It is used in the cuisines of Southeast Asia the way soy sauce is used in Chinese cuisine. This thin pungent liquid is rich in vitamins and is one of the most essential ingredients in Thai cooking. Its aroma may seem strong, but it gives layers of flavor. It is also placed on the table as a condiment at nearly every meal, either as is or mixed with sliced chilies and sometimes lime juice. There are many brands available and each country in Southeast Asia has its own version, from strong to mild. The fish sauces from Thailand and Vietnam are very mild compared to those from the Philippines, so choose your brand carefully.

Galanga: Also known as Laos, this root looks similar to common ginger. The flavor has a piny citrus quality. Like lemon grass, it is very finely chopped before using or sliced in large chunks, simmered in a sauce to infuse flavor and then removed. Galanga will keep for about a week in the fridge and can be frozen for up to one month. It is also available in dried pieces and in powdered form. Common ginger is a possible substitute, although the flavor is different.

Hoisin sauce: This Chinese bottled sauce has a dark reddish-brown color, a thick texture and a rich sweet flavor. It is made primarily from fermented soybeans and usually contains soybean paste, sugar, garlic and star anise. It will keep in the fridge for several months.

Kaffir lime and lime leaves: The kaffir lime tree is sought out more for the marvelous perfume and flavor of its distinctive double leaf than for the lime itself. Kaffir lime leaves are very finely shredded and added raw to many types of curries, soups and salads. The leaves are also used as a herb. The leaves freeze quite well and will keep their flavor for a few months if wrapped well before freezing. They are also available dried, but most of the perfume is lost in the drying process. The kaffir lime has a dark green, bumpy skin. There is almost no juice inside, but the lime is valued for its zest. Common lime juice and lime zest combined is the only possible substitute.

Lemon grass: This long slim bulb is used in all Southeast Asian cooking and it has a distinct citrus aroma and flavor. It is hard and fibrous, and it is necessary to chop off the root end and the top few inches. It is very finely chopped before cooking, or else it is chopped in large chunks, simmered in a liquid to infuse flavor and removed before serving. It will keep for about 10 days in the fridge or it can be frozen for up to a month. It is a perennial and will grow well indoors in a sunny warm location.

Long beans: These beans can grow to 3 feet (90 cm) in length but it is best to use younger, shorter ones, about a foot (30 cm) long. They are also called yard-long beans and snake beans. You will find them under the name *dow gok* in Chinese markets. They are crisp in texture and have a wonderful flavor similar to a cross between a green bean and asparagus. Common green beans make a good substitute.

Maggi seasoning sauce: This dark brown liquid is similar to soy sauce, but it is made from hydrolized vegetable protein instead of soybeans. It is a flavor enhancer that is available in most supermarkets. A possible substitute would be chicken or vegetable stock that is reduced by boiling until it has a very strong flavor.

Mung bean noodles: Bean thread noodles, or mung bean vermicelli are made from ground mung beans, the beans that are commonly used to make bean sprouts. They have a texture like wire when dry but when boiled or soaked in hot water they become soft, slippery and translucent. They are also called silver bean thread noodles, glass noodles or cellophane noodles. They're flavorless and take on the taste of their accompanying sauce or dressing. They are often used in salads or soups. Thin rice noodles could be substituted.

Palm sugar: A golden-brown compressed sugar made from the sap of coconut palms, it tastes similar to brown sugar, which is a good substitute. It can be purchased in the form of hard disks or in jars, where it has a texture like thick honey. It can be found in Indian markets, where it is called jaggery. It is added to sauces, curries and sweets.

Rice: Jasmine rice is commonly known as scented rice, fragrant rice or aromatic rice. It is a high-quality, long-grain white rice that has a world-famous reputation for appearance, flavor, texture and aroma. Both raw and cooked rice have the fragrance that is the reason for its name. This is the most commonly used rice in Thailand. **Sticky** or **glutinous rice** is an aptly named short, round-grain variety. The high gluten (a protein found in wheat flour) content is the reason it becomes sticky when cooked. In the north of Thailand, where it is formed into balls and eaten with fingers, it usually accompanies savory dishes like curry, but most frequently it is used for desserts. **Black rice** is a small, long-grained glutinous rice variety with a rich black color. Black rice is eaten in the north of Thailand with savory foods, but is more often used throughout the rest of the country (as well as Malaysia and Indonesia) for desserts, such as black rice pudding. **Red rice** is similar to whole-grain brown rice, but it has a rusty red color. It has a very hearty, nutty flavor and is excellent with a spicy curry. It requires more water and almost twice the cooking time of jasmine rice.

Rice noodles: These flat white noodles are made from rice flour. They are usually sold in three widths: wide (1 inch/2–3 cm) *sen yai*; narrow (1/4 inch/5 mm) *sen lek*; thin (1/16–1/8 inch/1 1/2–2 mm) *sen mi*. Fresh rice noodles are sold in the markets in Thailand, but in the West dried noodles are more common. Dried rice noodles need to be handled more delicately when soaking and cooking than wheat noodles. It is important not to use water that is too hot or to soak rice noodles for too long, because they will start to dissolve and get mushy.

Shallots: Considered to be the gourmet member of the onion family because of their mild, delicate flavor, shallots are very similar to green onions but develop in clusters of small bulbs rather than as individual onions. The flavor is like a cross between an onion and garlic, but milder than both. Asian red shallots are smaller than Western shallots. They have quite a pronounced flavor that is almost fruity rather than pungent. Ordinary shallots or the bottom of green onions can be substituted for Asian shallots.

Shrimp, dried: These are whole shrimp that have been dried in the sun. They are available in various sizes and qualities in most Asian markets. They are prized for their intense, concentrated flavor and are used in numerous ways, from stir-fry dishes to uncooked dipping sauces.

Shrimp paste: A very salty paste of sun-dried, salted shrimp, used in curry pastes, sauces, soups or stir-fries. Thai shrimp paste comes in small plastic jars and it has a very strong, fishy flavor and smell. It has the consistency and color of soft clay. Most countries in Southeast Asia have a version of shrimp paste, and they all taste different. A shrimp paste from Singapore, for example, would not be the right flavor to use in a Thai dish. The best substitute is anchovy paste.

Soy sauce: Light soy sauce is a Chinese-style soy sauce that is used in many different Thai dishes. The word light refers to the mild flavor and does not imply low fat or salt content. It can be used as a substitute for fish sauce in vegetarian dishes. **Dark soy sauce** has a very dark color and a rich caramelized flavor. It is slightly less salty than light soy sauce. Dark soy sauce is often used in noodle dishes and is common in marinades for meat and poultry. Dark soy sauce and light soy sauce are not interchangeable. **Sweet soy sauce** or *kecap manis* is a dark, very thick sauce from Indonesia that is usually used as a dip or condiment.

Szechuan peppercorns: These are not true peppercorns but the dried, small brown seeds of the prickly ash tree. These seeds are aromatic and spicy rather than hot. Szechuan peppercorns are usually toasted in a hot dry pan and then ground to a powder before being used.

Tamarind: The tamarind tree is believed to be a native of tropical East Africa, but it has long been cultivated in India. Today it is grown throughout the world in warm climates. It is used in Thai cooking primarily as a souring agent, like lime. The pod looks like an elongated peanut and it is the pulp around the seeds that is used. It has the texture of a date and a fruity sour taste, as it contains a lot of tartaric acid. Tamarind sold in stores is a brown sticky mass of pods, containing fiber and a number of seeds. The best tamarind comes from Petchaboon district, north of Bangkok; it is sweet enough to eat as a snack. It is usually tamarind water (page xx) that is used in cooking.

Thai basil: This fragrant member of the basil family is known as *bai kraprow* in Thailand. It is the most widely used of several different types of basil that are used in Thai dishes. It has dark green leaves and reddish purple stems. The flavor is similar to anise, and a good substitute is common Italian basil with a little anise powder.

Mail Order Sources for Thai Ingredients

Adriana's Caravan
409 Vanderbilt St.
Brooklyn, NY 11218
Tel: (800) 316-0820
E-mail: *adricara@aol.com*

Has a number of Thai staples.

Anzen Japanese Foods and Imports
736 Martin Luther King Jr. Blvd.
Portland, OR 97232
Tel: (503) 233-5111

Drop them a postcard to receive a listing of products. If it isn't on the list, they still might have it, so phone and ask.

Erawan Market
1463 University Ave.
Berkeley, CA 94702
Tel: (510) 849-9707
Fax: (650) 994-9896

Erawan offers a full range of Thai ingredients when available. They will sell you anything in the store that they can ship. This is where you can buy everything in one place.

Thai Grocery
5014 N. Broadway St.
Chicago, IL 60640
Tel: (773) 561-5345

They will sell you anything in their store that they can ship.

Uwajimaya
519 – 6th Ave. South
Seattle, WA 98104
Tel: (206) 624-6248
Fax: (206) 624-6915
E-mail: *harvey@uwajimaya.com*

Free catalog: (800) 889-1928.
Their catalog has Mae Ploy curry pastes (a good brand), tamarind, kapi (shrimp paste), palm sugar, wet tamarind, Chaokoh Coconut Milk, dried rice noodles, and some dried spices. You can also order non-catalog items that are in the store. (*Note:* you cannot order online, and their website does not list products.)

The following Internet addresses will take you to websites where all the essential Thai ingredients are available by mail:

http://www.templeofthai.com/thai_marketplace/
thai_marketplace.html

http://www.importfood.com/

158

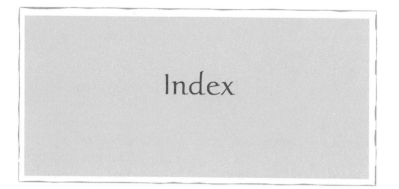

Index

apples: Chicken, Prawn and Fruit Salad 60

Apricot Ginger Dipping Sauce 20

asparagus: Chili Garlic Prawns with Asparagus 80

Baa Wan's Squid Stir-fry 78

bamboo shoots: Coconut-Lime Green Beans and
      Bamboo Shoots 116

   Lettuce Wraps 44

   Spinach and Mushroom Potstickers 31

bananas: Banana Coconut Candy 147

   Banana Ginger Squares 148

   Banana Lime Sauté 141

   Banana Mango Cake 150

   Banana Whiskey Cream Sauce 140

   Chocolate Banana Coconut Cake 151

   Sticky Rice and Banana Grilled in Banana
      Leaves 143

   Tropical Trifle 144

Bangkok Coconut Rice Noodles 132

Bangkok Street Vendor Rice Noodle Stir-fry 134

Barbecued Duck and Mushroom Fresh Spring Rolls
   40

beans, green: Chili Garlic Beans with Cashews 115

   Coconut Curry Chicken with Ginger and Eggplant
      105

   Coconut-Lime Green Beans and Bamboo Shoots
      116

   Fish and Vegetable Patties 33

   Green Bean Salad with Coconut Milk Dressing 65

beans, long: Chili Garlic Beans with Cashews 115

bean sprouts: Bangkok Coconut Rice Noodles 132

   Bangkok Street Vendor Rice Noodle Stir-fry 134

   Bean Sprout and Scallion Stir-fry 119

   Dried Shrimp (or Chicken) Paad Thai 135

   Leaf-wrapped Rice Noodles with Savories 45

   Shiitake Mushroom Rice Noodle Stir-fry 131

   Stir-fried Red Curry Mango Vegetables 117

   Thai Spring Rolls 39

   Tiger Prawn Paad Thai 136

bean thread noodles: Lemon Grass Beef Salad 64

   Southern Thai Bean Thread Noodle and Chicken
      Salad 62

beef: Lemon Grass Beef Salad 64

   Lettuce Wraps 44

   Spicy Street Satay 35

bok choy: Stir-fried Red Curry Mango Vegetables 117

broccoli: Country-Style Hot and Sour Soup 57

   Peanut Sesame Orange Chicken 106

cabbage: Leaf-wrapped Rice Noodles with Savories 45

   Northern Thai Shrimp Salad 63

   Roasted Rock Fish With Coconut and Mango 74

   Som Tam Green Papaya Salad 66

   Thai Spring Rolls 39

cake: Banana Mango Cake 150

   Chocolate Banana Coconut Cake 151

candy: Banana Coconut Candy 147

carrots: Northern Thai Shrimp Salad 63

   Peanut Sesame Noodle Salad 67

cauliflower: Country-Style Hot and Sour Soup 57

Chiang Mai Noodles 130
chicken: Chiang Mai Noodles 130
 Chicken and Cashew Fried Rice 126
 Chicken and Coconut Milk Soup 50
 Chicken and Mushrooms in Green Coconut Curry 104
 Chicken, Prawn and Fruit Salad 60
 Chicken and Red Peppers in Red Coconut Curry Sauce 94
 Chicken and Snow Peas with Curry Cream Pasta 137
 Chicken Wings in Lemon Grass Red Wine Sauce 42
 Chopped Chicken Salad 61
 Coconut Curry Chicken with Ginger and Eggplant 105
 Coconut Lemon Grass Baked Chicken 102
 Coconut Marinated Chicken Satay 37
 Coriander Broth with Prawn and Pork Dumplings 53
 Country-Style Hot and Sour Soup 57
 Dried Shrimp (or Chicken) Paad Thai 135
 Herb Glazed Chicken 103
 Lettuce Wraps 44
 Lime and Tamarind Chicken 93
 Massaman Chicken Curry 92
 Minced Chicken and Water Chestnut Dumplings 28
 Northern Thai Whiskey Marinated Chicken Wings 41
 Northern-Style Marinated Chicken with Sweet Tomato Chutney 98
 Peanut Sesame Orange Chicken 106
 Pineapple Chicken and Cashews in Banana Leaves 91
 Rama Spinach Chicken Curry 95
 Roasted Chili Paste Chicken and Peanuts in Banana Leaves 96
 Southern Thai Bean Thread Noodle and Chicken Salad 62
 Spicy Chicken, Basil and Pepper Stir-fry 99

chicken (cont.):
 Spicy Cilantro Roast Chicken with Honey Lime Sauce 101
 Spicy Mint Chicken 97
 Spicy Street Satay 35
 Thai Chicken Stock 25
 Thai Roasted Vegetable and Chicken Soup 48
 Thai Spring Rolls 39
 Thai Whiskey Peppercorn Marinated Chicken 100
 Tom Yam Chicken Soup 52
chili flakes, toasting 135
Chili Garlic Beans with Cashews 115
Chili Garlic Prawns with Asparagus 80
chili paste: Roasted Chili Paste 12
chili sauce: Quick Sweet and Sour Chili Sauce 21
 Sweet Chili Sauce 22
Chocolate Banana Coconut Cake 151
Chopped Chicken Salad 61
coconut, toasting 123
coconut: Banana Coconut Candy 147
 Banana Ginger Squares 148
 Banana Mango Cake 150
 Chocolate Banana Coconut Cake 151
 Coconut Ginger Chocolate Brownies 149
 Eggplant Stuffed with Coconut and Cilantro 111
 Ginger and Mushroom Baked Coconut Rice 128
 Ginger-Infused Toasted Coconut Jasmine Rice 123
 Leaf-wrapped Rice Noodles with Savories 45
 Mango Cream Tarts 152
 Yam and Sesame Patties 34
coconut cream: Curried Vegetables in Banana Leaves 118
 Gingered Black Rice Pudding 146
 Salmon Baked in Banana Leaves 73
Coconut Cream Pudding 145
Coconut Curry Chicken with Ginger and Eggplant 105
Coconut Ginger Chocolate Brownies 149
Coconut Ginger Sauce 17
Coconut Lemon Grass Baked Chicken 102
Coconut-Lime Green Beans and Bamboo Shoots 116
Coconut Marinated Chicken Satay 37

coconut milk: Bangkok Coconut Rice Noodles 132
    Chicken and Coconut Milk Soup 50
    Chicken and Mushrooms in Green Coconut Curry 104
    Chicken and Red Peppers in Red Coconut Curry Sauce 94
    Coconut Cream Pudding 145
    Coconut Curry Chicken with Ginger and Eggplant 105
    Coconut Marinated Chicken Satay 37
    Eggplant and Potato in Green Coconut Curry Sauce 112
    Green Bean Salad with Coconut Milk Dressing 65
    Khanom Krok Coconut Dumplings 29
    Lime and Tamarind Chicken 93
    Massaman Chicken Curry 92
    Monkfish in Green Coconut Curry Sauce 75
    Rama Spinach Chicken Curry 95
    Red Snapper and Prawns in Lemon Grass Coconut Curry Sauce 79
    Smoked Oyster Coconut Sauce 24
    Steamed Seafood Custard 87
    Sticky Rice and Mango 142
    Yellow Curry Sauce 18
Coriander Broth with Prawn and Pork Dumplings 53
corn: Peanut Sesame Orange Chicken 106
    Sweet Corn Patties 32
    Thai Basil and Sweet Corn 120
Country-Style Hot and Sour Soup 57
crab: Sanit's Sweet Chili Green Mango Dip 46
Creamy Peanut Sauce 13
cucumber: Chopped Chicken Salad 61
    Cucumber Chili Salad 69
    Leaf-wrapped Rice Noodles with Savories 45
    Lemon Grass Beef Salad 64
    Lettuce Wraps 44
    Northern Thai Shrimp Salad 63
Curried Spinach with Tofu and Cashews 114
Curried Vegetables in Banana Leaves 118
curry paste, freezing 9

curry paste: Green Curry Paste 9
    Massaman Curry Paste 11
    Panaeng Curry Paste 10
    Red Curry Paste 8
curry sauce: Yellow Curry Sauce 18

dips: Green Peppercorn Dip 20
    Sanit's Sweet Chili Green Mango Dip 46
    Spinach and Peanut Dip 38
dipping sauce: Apricot Ginger Dipping Sauce 20
    Dipping Sauce for Dumplings 19
Dried Shrimp (or Chicken) Paad Thai 135
Drunkard's Noodles 133
duck: Barbecued Duck and Mushroom Fresh Spring Rolls 40
    Duck and Mushroom Potstickers with Apricot Ginger Dipping Sauce 30
    Lime and Honey Roasted Duck 90
dumplings: Coriander Broth with Prawn and Pork Dumplings 53
    Khanom Krok Coconut Dumplings 29
    Minced Chicken and Water Chestnut Dumplings 28

egg noodles: Chiang Mai Noodles 130
    Egg Noodles with Thai Herb Pesto 129
    Peanut Sesame Noodle Salad 67
eggplant: Coconut Curry Chicken with Ginger and Eggplant 105
    Eggplant and Potato in Green Coconut Curry Sauce 112
    Eggplant Stuffed with Coconut and Cilantro 111
    Keow's Roasted Eggplant Salad 68
eggs: Bangkok Street Vendor Rice Noodle Stir-fry 134
    Chicken and Cashew Fried Rice 126
    Dried Shrimp (or Chicken) Paad Thai 135
    Keow's Roasted Eggplant Salad 68
    Steamed Seafood Custard 87
    Tiger Prawn Paad Thai 136

Fish and Vegetable Patties 33
fish sauce: Nam Pla Prig 18
fish: Grilled Pomfret with Tamarind Chili Sauce 76
    Monkfish in Green Coconut Curry Sauce 75
    Red Snapper and Prawns in Lemon Grass Coconut
        Curry Sauce 79
    Roasted Rock Fish With Coconut and Mango 74
    Salmon Baked in Banana Leaves 73
    Salmon in Rice Paper Wraps with Coconut Ginger
        Sauce 72
    Salmon, Tamarind and Ginger Soup 55
    Steamed Seafood Custard 87
5-Spice Powder 90

garlic, roasting 65
Ginger Cream Sauce 23
Gingered Black Rice Pudding 146
Ginger-Infused Toasted Coconut Jasmine Rice 123
Ginger and Mushroom Baked Coconut Rice 128
Green Bean Salad with Coconut Milk Dressing 65
Green Curry Paste 9
Green Peppercorn Dip 20
Grilled Pomfret with Tamarind Chili Sauce 76
Grilled Squid with Tamarind Chili Sauce 77

Herbed Prawn and Vegetable Soup 54
Herbed and Sweetened Prawns 43
Herb Glazed Chicken 103
Honey Lime Sauce 17

Jasmine Rice 122

Keow's Roasted Eggplant Salad 68
Khanom Krok Coconut Dumplings 29

Leaf-wrapped Rice Noodles with Savories 45
Lemon Grass Beef Salad 64
Lemon Grass Broth 26
Lemon Grass Curried Mussels 84
Lemon Grass Risotto 124
Lettuce Wraps 44

Lime and Honey Roasted Duck 90
Lime and Tamarind Chicken 93

mangos: Banana Mango Cake 150
    Gingered Black Rice Pudding 146
    Mango Coconut Custard Filling 152
    Mango Cream Tarts 152
    Mango Lime Sauce 140
    Roasted Rock Fish With Coconut and Mango 74
    Sanit's Sweet Chili Green Mango Dip 46
    Seared Scallops and Basil Mango Sauce 85
    Sticky Rice and Mango 142
    Stir-fried Red Curry Mango Vegetables 117
    Tropical Trifle 144
Massaman Chicken Curry 92
Massaman Curry Paste 11
Minced Chicken and Water Chestnut Dumplings
    28
Monkfish in Green Coconut Curry Sauce 75
mortar and pestle 5
mushrooms: Barbecued Duck and Mushroom Fresh
       Spring Rolls 40
    Chicken and Cashew Fried Rice 126
    Chicken and Mushrooms in Green Coconut Curry
       104
    Duck and Mushroom Potstickers with Apricot
       Ginger Dipping Sauce 30
    Ginger and Mushroom Baked Coconut Rice 128
    Mushroom Satay 109
    Pineapple Fried Rice 125
    Rachini's Mushroom Stir-fry 110
    Shiitake Mushroom Rice Noodle Stir-fry 131
    Southern Thai Bean Thread Noodle and Chicken
       Salad 62
    Spinach and Mushroom Potstickers 31
    Thai Roasted Vegetable and Chicken Soup 48
    Tom Yam Chicken Soup 52
    Tom Yam Prawn Soup 51
    Vegetarian Tom Yam Soup 56
mussels: Lemon Grass Curried Mussels 84

Nam Pla Prig 18

noodle dishes. *See* bean thread noodles, egg noodles, rice noodles

Northern-Style Marinated Chicken with Sweet Tomato Chutney 98

Northern Thai Shrimp Salad 63

Northern Thai Whiskey Marinated Chicken Wings 41

oranges: Chicken, Prawn and Fruit Salad 60

oysters: Smoked Oyster Coconut Sauce 24

Panaeng Curry Paste 10

papaya: Som Tam Green Papaya Salad 66
    Tropical Trifle 144

pasta: Chicken and Snow Peas with Curry Cream Pasta 137

patties: Fish and Vegetable Patties 33
    Sweet Corn Patties 32
    Yam and Sesame Patties 34

peanut sauce: Creamy Peanut Sauce 13
    Pineapple Peanut Sauce 14
    Tamarind Peanut Sauce 16
    Thai Hoisin Peanut Sauce 15

Peanut Sesame Noodle Salad 67

Peanut Sesame Orange Chicken 106

peppers, bell: Baa Wan's Squid Stir-fry 78
    Chicken and Mushrooms in Green Coconut Curry 104
    Chicken and Red Peppers in Red Coconut Curry Sauce 94
    Cucumber Chili Salad 69
    Curried Spinach with Tofu and Cashews 114
    Drunkard's Noodles 133
    Herb Glazed Chicken 103
    Monkfish in Green Coconut Curry Sauce 75
    Northern Thai Shrimp Salad 63
    Peanut Sesame Orange Chicken 106
    Phuket Prawns 83
    Spicy Chicken, Basil and Pepper Stir-fry 99
    Stir-fried Red Curry Mango Vegetables 117

pesto: Thai Herb Pesto Sauce 81

Phuket Prawns 83

pineapple: Banana Mango Cake 150
    Pineapple Chicken and Cashews in Banana Leaves 91
    Pineapple Fried Rice 125
    Pineapple Peanut Sauce 14

pork: Coriander Broth with Prawn and Pork Dumplings 53
    Lettuce Wraps 44
    Pork Satay 36
    Spicy Street Satay 35
    Thai Spring Rolls 39

potatoes: Eggplant and Potato in Green Coconut Curry Sauce 112
    Yam and Sesame Patties 34

potstickers: Duck and Mushroom Potstickers with Apricot Ginger Dipping Sauce 30
    Spinach and Mushroom Potstickers 31

prawns: Chicken, Prawn and Fruit Salad 60
    Chili Garlic Prawns with Asparagus 80
    Coriander Broth with Prawn and Pork Dumplings 53
    Country-Style Hot and Sour Soup 57
    Herbed Prawn and Vegetable Soup 54
    Herbed and Sweetened Prawns 43
    Phuket Prawns 83
    Prawns with Ginger Cream Sauce 82
    Red Snapper and Prawns in Lemon Grass Coconut Curry Sauce 79
    Steamed Seafood Custard 87
    Tiger Prawn and Basil Fried Rice 127
    Tiger Prawn Paad Thai 136
    Tiger Prawns with Thai Herb Pesto Sauce 81
    Tom Yam Prawn Soup 51

pudding: Coconut Cream Pudding 145
    Gingered Black Rice Pudding 146

Quick Sweet and Sour Chili Sauce 21

Rachini's Mushroom Stir-fry 110

Rama Spinach Chicken Curry 95

Red Curry Paste 8
Red Snapper and Prawns in Lemon Grass Coconut
    Curry Sauce 79
rice noodles, preparing 132
rice noodles: Bangkok Coconut Rice Noodles 132
    Bangkok Street Vendor Rice Noodle Stir-fry 134
    Dried Shrimp (or Chicken) Paad Thai 135
    Drunkard's Noodles 133
    Leaf-wrapped Rice Noodles with Savories 45
    Lemon Grass Beef Salad 64
    Peanut Sesame Noodle Salad 67
    Shiitake Mushroom Rice Noodle Stir-fry 131
    Tiger Prawn Paad Thai 136
Roasted Chili Paste 12
Roasted Chili Paste Chicken and Peanuts in Banana
    Leaves 96
Roasted Rock Fish With Coconut and Mango 74
roasting garlic 65

salmon: Salmon Baked in Banana Leaves 73
    Salmon in Rice Paper Wraps with Coconut Ginger
        Sauce 72
    Salmon, Tamarind and Ginger Soup 55
Sanit's Sweet Chili Green Mango Dip 46
satay: Coconut Marinated Chicken Satay 37
    Mushroom Satay 109
    Pork Satay 36
    Spicy Street Satay 35
scallops: Seared Scallops and Basil Mango Sauce 85
    Steamed Seafood Custard 87
    Whiskey and Coconut Marinated Seared Scallops
        86
shellfish: Baa Wan's Squid Stir-fry 78
    Chicken, Prawn and Fruit Salad 60
    Chili Garlic Prawns with Asparagus 80
    Coriander Broth with Prawn and Pork Dumplings
        53
    Country-Style Hot and Sour Soup 57
    Dried Shrimp (or Chicken) Paad Thai 135
    Grilled Squid with Tamarind Chili Sauce 77
    Herbed Prawn and Vegetable Soup 54

shellfish (cont.):
    Herbed and Sweetened Prawns 43
    Lemon Grass Curried Mussels 84
    Northern Thai Shrimp Salad 63
    Phuket Prawns 83
    Prawns with Ginger Cream Sauce 82
    Red Snapper and Prawns in Lemon Grass Coconut
        Curry Sauce 79
    Sanit's Sweet Chili Green Mango Dip 46
    Seared Scallops and Basil Mango Sauce 85
    Steamed Seafood Custard 87
    Thai Shrimp and Jasmine Rice Soup 49
    Thai Spring Rolls 39
    Tiger Prawn and Basil Fried Rice 127
    Tiger Prawn Paad Thai 136
    Tiger Prawns with Thai Herb Pesto Sauce 81
    Tom Yam Prawn Soup 51
    Whiskey and Coconut Marinated Seared Scallops
        86
Shiitake Mushroom Rice Noodle Stir-fry 131
shrimp: Dried Shrimp (or Chicken) Paad Thai 135
    Herbed Prawn and Vegetable Soup 54
    Northern Thai Shrimp Salad 63
    Sanit's Sweet Chili Green Mango Dip 46
    Thai Shrimp and Jasmine Rice Soup 49
    Thai Spring Rolls 39
Smoked Oyster Coconut Sauce 24
snapper: Red Snapper and Prawns in Lemon Grass
        Coconut Curry Sauce 79
    Roasted Rock Fish With Coconut and Mango 74
snow peas: Chicken and Snow Peas with Curry
        Cream Pasta 137
    Southern Thai Bean Thread Noodle and Chicken
        Salad 62
Som Tam Green Papaya Salad 66
Southern Thai Bean Thread Noodle and Chicken
    Salad 62
Spicy Chicken, Basil and Pepper Stir-fry 99
Spicy Cilantro Roast Chicken with Honey Lime Sauce
    101
Spicy Mint Chicken 97

Spicy Street Satay 35
spinach: Barbecued Duck and Mushroom Fresh
        Spring Rolls 40
    Curried Spinach with Tofu and Cashews 114
    Rama Spinach Chicken Curry 95
    Spinach and Mushroom Potstickers 31
    Spinach and Peanut Dip 38
    Stir-fried Spinach with Salted Soybeans 113
spring rolls: Barbecued Duck and Mushroom Fresh
        Spring Rolls 40
    Thai Spring Rolls 39
squares: Banana Ginger Squares 148
    Coconut Ginger Chocolate Brownies 149
squid: Baa Wan's Squid Stir-fry 78
    Grilled Squid with Tamarind Chili Sauce 77
Steamed Seafood Custard 87
Sticky Rice and Banana Grilled in Banana Leaves 143
Sticky Rice and Mango 142
Stir-fried Red Curry Mango Vegetables 117
Stir-fried Spinach with Salted Soybeans 113
stir-fry techniques 5
stock: Lemon Grass Broth 26
    Thai Chicken Stock 25
sui choy: Roasted Rock Fish With Coconut and
        Mango 74
    Som Tam Green Papaya Salad 66
    Stir-fried Red Curry Mango Vegetables 117
Sweet Chili Sauce 22
Sweet Corn Patties 32
Sweet Hot Tamarind Sauce 16
Sweet Tomato Chutney 98

Tamarind Chili Sauce 76
Tamarind Peanut Sauce 16
tamarind water 48
tarts: Mango Cream Tarts 152
Thai Basil and Sweet Corn 120
Thai Black or Red Rice 122
Thai Chicken Stock 25
Thai Herb Pesto Sauce 81
Thai Hoisin Peanut Sauce 15

Thai Roasted Vegetable and Chicken Soup 48
Thai Shrimp and Jasmine Rice Soup 49
Thai Spring Rolls 39
Thai Whiskey Peppercorn Marinated Chicken 100
Tiger Prawn and Basil Fried Rice 127
Tiger Prawn Paad Thai 136
Tiger Prawns with Thai Herb Pesto Sauce 81
toasted rice powder 61
tofu: Bangkok Street Vendor Rice Noodle Stir-fry 134
    Curried Spinach with Tofu and Cashews 114
    Dried Shrimp (or Chicken) Paad Thai 135
    Tiger Prawn Paad Thai 136
Tom Yam Chicken Soup 52
Tom Yam Prawn Soup 51
Tropical Trifle 144

Vegetables in Lemon Grass Broth 108
Vegetarian Tom Yam Soup 56

Whiskey and Coconut Marinated Seared Scallops 86
wraps: Leaf-wrapped Rice Noodles with Savories 45
    Lettuce Wraps 44

Yam and Sesame Patties 34
Yellow Curry Sauce 18

zucchini: Stir-fried Red Curry Mango Vegetables 117

About the Author

How did Nathan Hyam, a chef born in New York City, come to be known as "the Thai Guy"? After combining his love of food and teaching with his experience working as Head Chef-Instructor at the Picasso Café, a restaurant-training program for youth at risk, Nathan traded his apron for a suitcase and went on a sabbatical with his wife. They found themselves in Thailand and quickly became immersed in the scents and flavors of Thai cuisine. A decade later, after many Thai cooking courses, mentoring by acclaimed Thai chefs, and more travels in Asia, Nathan is one of the preeminent chefs in Vancouver specializing in Thai cuisine. His popular cooking classes, peppered with tips on how to replicate authentic Thai cuisine in Western kitchens, are the hottest ticket in town. *New Thai Cuisine* is his first cookbook.